LEADING BEYOND A CRISIS

A Conversation About What's Next

Ben Baker
&
Claire Chandler

Leading Beyond A Crisis
A Conversation About What's Next

Hard Cover Version ISBN: 978-1-7772563-0-2
Soft Cover Version ISBN: 978-1-7772563-1-9
Digital Version ISBN: 978-1-7772563-3-3

Publisher:
Your Brand Marketing, a division of CMYK Solutions Inc.
3246 Regent Street
Richmond, BC
V7E 2M9
Canada

Table of Contents

Foreword

A LEADER'S REFLECTIONS ON *LEADING BEYOND A CRISIS*

What I love about *Leading Beyond A Crisis* is that it's a conversation between Ben and Claire. Their backgrounds, exchange of ideas and real-world experiences really help to deliver the message, and the examples they use help readers visualize what leadership is meant to be.

I have never seen or been a part of leadership that does any of the things that this book promotes. Frankly, I don't know if I am ever going to see this in my working life. I'd love to be part of an organization that uses these principles as its backbone. In my almost 30-year work history, I have only dealt with "leaders" who are on a power trip and have huge egos that need to be stroked by their employees. They all want "yes men" and do not want to see or look outside of that box— as if they are the only ones who can generate, develop or implement new ideas. I have never been empowered to make decisions—and I ran two companies for 10-plus years. After reading this, I now realize that they do not have the ability to lead. They use their position to have their employees serve them, not the other way around. They want to be in control, and in most cases, they do not trust their employees, which begs the question: Why did they hire them in the first place? I think it's sad, and I think it needs to change.

I really believe that leaders should be leading in the way that Ben and Claire describe. Getting the most out of your employees means getting them involved. They must have a say, or there will never be any buy-in at any level.

I'd love to be able to lead like this. I do what I can to implement these principles into my daily work and communication habits. I don't know what difference I will ultimately make, but I still try to lead this way. I'm committed to continue to learn, and to inspire others. I'll do my best.

—*Dan Bigger, Director Sales & Marketing*

Introduction

WELCOME TO THE NEW WORLD

Welcome to *Leading Beyond A Crisis: A Conversation About What's Next.*

This book is an adaptation of a series of video conversations that took place in the spring of 2020. These conversations were designed to help leaders look beyond the serious, near-term challenges they were facing because of the global pandemic, and create business environments that thrive over the long term; to lead people beyond the anxiety and stress; and to bring them through the tunnel toward the light, so they can ask, "What's next?"

Part of what we wanted to accomplish was to get people to pick their heads up and start looking toward the horizon once again. Unfortunately, it is so easy for everyone to put their heads down in the muck and worry so much about the current state that they forget to build for the future. This was the reason we wanted to have that conversation: to bring people out of the muck and toward the light.

❝We started these conversations to help leaders pull themselves and their people through this time of unprecedented crisis, and to remind them that there is a future to build.❞

We are facing a new reality. The way we did business in the past is changing. How we communicate with our people, interact with our vendors, and engage with our clients will all change—probably for the better. We are going to be more creative and more innovative and find different ways to add value. That is what this conversation is all about.

What's your story? What are the conversations you need to be having, with whom, how and why? At the end of each chapter, we offer questions to help you guide those conversations.

Be the leader you are meant to be.

Start the conversation here.

—Ben Baker [BB] and Claire Chandler [CC]

EPISODE 1

TIME TO GET "STUPID SIMPLE"

CC: This pandemic is a shared experience unlike anything the world has ever seen before. It is a globally shared experience—and we should take some comfort, some solidarity in that. But merely surviving COVID-19 cannot be anyone's brand story going forward. That cannot be what you build a business around. Because if all you focus on is getting through this crisis, you won't actually thrive as a business. That's the stark reality. We don't want this to be a "doom and gloom" conversation, but we do want to be mindful of the reality that a lot of businesses will not survive this crisis. A trusted colleague of mine pointed out recently that if you were doing very well in 2019 when the economy was booming, but you really didn't have much figured out, you were getting by on luck more than skill; this crisis really rocked you back on your heels. We no longer live in a world of "survival of the fittest"; we are now in a time of "survival of the adaptable." The businesses that come through this crisis and look for the opportunities to become more efficient, stay effective, maintain the core of their workforce and the core of who they are and why they are in business— those are the companies and leaders that will actually thrive at the end of this and be looked to as the examples in their industry.

❝We no longer live in a world of "survival of the fittest"; we are now in a time of "survival of the adaptable."❞

BB: Exactly. How many companies that are out there today, that were doing really, really well in 2019, were doing okay in 2009? We're dealing with a period of time where we've had 10 plus years of incredible growth. An amazing amount of companies have been growing. A lot of businesses have been developed. And the people who lead them—the CEOs, the VPs, the managers—within these companies have grown up in a position where they've always had year-after-year growth and double-digit growth. But suddenly, the world has changed. And the companies that I've been talking to that were around in 2008—the same year I started my company, Your Brand Marketing, to give everybody some context. Thank God for great customers, that's all I can say. But the people who were around pre-2008, through the crisis that happened there, I'm having completely different conversations with than the companies that were founded and built post-2010, 2011, because they've never seen this. They've never seen a downturn. They've never been in a position where they've said, "I have to do massive layoffs. I need to change my business model, refocus, be creative, and communicate in a completely different way with my customers." And yes, 2020 is a completely different type of meltdown than 2008 was—while that one was strictly financial, this one has the pandemic on top of it—so there are differences. But the reality is, this is not the last one. We are going to have another recession, another meltdown sometime in the future. And the companies that can futureproof themselves, the companies that can say, "We're going to have good markets, we're going to have bad markets. We need to be prepared for all of these things and have the systems in place to be able to push ourselves forward"—those are the ones that are going to survive and thrive. The ones that are saying, "This is a deep dark hole, but there are opportunities that can come out of this"—those are the conversations we all need to be having.

❝The companies that can futureproof themselves… are the ones that are going to survive and thrive. ❞

CC: As you said, this is not the first crisis that you or I have seen in business. For a lot of businesses that are relatively young, this IS their first real crisis. Because they were riding on a wave of prosperity for close to a decade, they are ill-prepared for how to pull themselves and their workforce through this. I'm reminded of not only the economic downturn—some called it a crash—of over a decade ago, but I live on the East Coast, where in 2012 Superstorm Sandy had a devastating effect on people, both personally and professionally, as well as financially. These sorts of crises—whether they are regional, national or global—come around from time to time. This will certainly not be the last one. One of the things that it does is it wipes the slate clean. When I use that phrase, a lot of people see its negative implication, that it wipes people out. That's not what I mean by that. What I mean is this: A crisis forces businesses and leaders to get really "stupid simple" in the ways that they communicate, and in the ways that they get from A to B. You talked about processes: "How do we keep the lights on, the business running, our people paid" are very simple decisions when a crisis like this occurs. So looking at these as opportunities—that's where leaders, real leaders, and leading businesses, will emerge from this crisis the stronger for it.

❝A crisis forces businesses and leaders to get really "stupid simple" in the ways that they communicate, and in the ways that they get from A to B.❞

BB: I remember having a conversation with somebody a year ago. We're a small company—we're not a multimillion-dollar company, we're not a billion-dollar corporation—so you have to scale this conversation to think about it. But somebody said "Well, what would happen if your house burned down or your business broke down or whatever?" I said, "You know what? I'd go to Best Buy, I'd buy a laptop, and within 20 minutes I could probably be back up and running." My entire life is on the cloud. Everything is backed up on a regular basis on two different backup systems that are both cloud-based; I do have an external backup on my hard drive at the office, but I also have cloud backup happening at any given time, to make sure that we're taken care of. It's little, simple things like that. Can you survive a crash, a crisis? What happens if a hard drive fails? We're not just talking a pandemic. We're not just talking—God forbid—acts of terrorism. We all need to be prepared for the unexpected. It's the companies that can say, "May this never happen, but if it does, we've got policies and procedures to deal with this." And they practice them, augment them, challenge them, figure them out, and then test them and think, "Well, that didn't work; now let's go forward from here." The companies that are constantly thinking about "what if," and have been thinking "what if" for a while, are probably going to do better through this than the companies that have just gone off on a lick and a prayer and said, "We're making money, so we're not going to worry about it." Those are the companies right now that need to take a really quick step back and do an audit of what's working, what's not working, what systems they have in place, what systems they're missing, what skill sets they have within their current workforce, and how they utilize those skills to their advantage. There are people in your office who have skills that you probably don't even realize. The more you ask, "Who can do what? What are the things that we can do? How can we pivot from where we are and be able to come out of this?"— those are the companies that are going to do better in the short, medium and long term than the companies that are throwing up their hands and asking, "Where's the government assistance?"

❝The companies that are constantly thinking about "what if," and have been thinking "what if" for a while, are probably going to do better through this.❞

CC: The term that pops up for me is "lazy success." Businesses that have been riding on this wave of prosperity, and never disaster-planning—because their attitude is, "Why would we waste time and energy on a disaster that may never come?"—have been lucky. It's not just the large, global companies that can take a meteor strike of this kind and still survive, even if they have to close down a division; companies of any size can either fold or come out of this stronger. You used the Best Buy example: If your hard drive crashes, if you lose all your files, etc., your disaster plan for your physical assets is in place. That's pretty basic. But for a lot of companies, it's a basic they overlook. It's the WHAT: Let's make sure we've got the WHAT handled and contingency-planned. And the processes, the HOW we're going to get from A to B, have to be backed up, bulletproofed and battle-tested. The third one I would add is the WHO. The companies that have built up very good equity—not only internally, because they have very strong workplace cultures and loyal employees, but also a good reputation with the customers and the clients they serve—can draw upon that equity during tough times. This is a global crisis, so it's a little bit different because EVERYONE is hurting to some degree. But I can remember a time, several years ago, when my mother-in-law suddenly became gravely ill. Of course, my husband and I dropped everything and went to Texas to be with her. We ended up being away from our businesses for about a month, without pre-planning it. My husband is part of a very big company; he was able to do a lot of things remotely. And I was able not just to survive, but to come out of that stronger as a business owner, because I had extremely loyal, understanding, compassionate clients who said, "We get it; we're here. If you need a little extra time on a deadline or you need to communicate a little bit less right now, we understand why." It's that sort of equity that you build up as a business over time, internally and externally, that will help you through most disasters.

BB: That's built on open and direct communication, not trying to sugarcoat things, and saying, "Look, this is where we are." Asking your customer, "How can we help get our accounts receivable paid more quickly?" Asking your vendors, "Money's a little tight right now; how can we work together to make sure you get paid, but do it in a way that's not going to kill me?" How do you work with your banks? I just did this; I just had a conversation with my bank and said, "For 120 days, can we bump up my line of credit?" And in 120 days we have a handshake agreement that we're going to reevaluate it. It puts them in a temporary position where they're not raising my line of credit "willy nilly" or just carte blanche; it's for a limited amount of time, and it's for a limited amount. But it's that little extra that might help me out and be the difference between being in a total cash crunch and being just fine. So it's those open conversations that we have that are really, really important.

CC: In that example, you just demonstrated a lesson that all leaders can learn, which is the value of being vulnerable. Leaders are expected to have all the answers, to know how to get through every crisis, and to know how to succeed with their business. They put the most pressure on themselves. So in a time of crisis, whether it's global or local, choose to show vulnerability—to say to a bank, for example, "I need a little bit more help here, I need a little bit more leeway, etc."—versus the hubris of "If I admit that I need a little bit of a window, that's a failure." If you had taken that tack, you likely would not have made it through the storm. One of the key crossroads that leaders are at right now—who find themselves in these types of crises—is that choice between hubris and vulnerability. You can be vulnerable to your partners, your employees and your stakeholders in a way that doesn't show weakness, but shows humanity.

QUESTION:

What is the biggest challenge you are facing right now, and what have you learned about yourself in trying to overcome it?

_____

_____

_____

_____

_____

_____

_____

_____

_____

EPISODE 2

LEADERS BEING VULNERABLE

BB: We are absolutely in a new normal, and we need to talk about it. We need to know how we are going to survive and how we're going to thrive as leaders, as businesses, as people going forward. Because this is not going to last forever. This is not the first crisis the world has been in. We've been in many crises before; we're going to be in lots of crises moving forward. It's the companies that understand how to move forward through this, and understand how to build the best practices to be able to put themselves in the position to succeed, that are going to succeed. In our last episode, Claire, you ended off talking about vulnerability, and I think that's a great place to start.

CC: We talked about how important it is for business leaders to make the right turn at that fork in the road, between showing hubris and showing vulnerability. Leaders have so much pressure from the outside, and so much pressure from the voices in their own head, that they have to have all the answers, that they have to have all the solutions, whether it is a crisis or whether it's smooth sailing. But in a global pandemic like we are going through right now, NO ONE has all the answers, because none of us has ever been through something exactly like this. That is the reality. We are all learning as we go, and we are adapting as we go—at least the businesses and the leaders who are truly open to learning as they go. Learning to me is a key component as well. It's the companies, the businesses, but specifically the leaders who both learn and lean through this, who will come through the other side. I'll go a little bit deeper on that. Learning through this crisis how to do the job more efficiently— we talked last time about doing the necessary things to keep the lights on, the bills paid, your employees paid, etc.—but also learning as you go: What does this mean for the future of our company—not for the "now," but for the FUTURE of our company? What have we gone without since shifting to remote work, limiting travel and downsizing group interactions? Were any of those shifts truly sacrifices? And learning from that and saying, "When we get through this crisis"—and let me end the suspense for you: we will get through this crisis—but at the end of it, is any truly forward-thinking business going to revert to business as usual? If you are, I think that's a huge mistake. But it's completely unrealistic to think any business is NOT going to learn from this and just go back to business as usual. First of all, it's not going to be so easy to flip that switch backwards.

BB: It's that genie back in the bottle—it just doesn't go in that easily.

CC: Absolutely! She's got a big, full skirt that does not go back in the bottle the way it popped out. So there's that learning component. And the LEANING component comes back to this vulnerability that we spoke of. Vulnerability is not the same as weakness. I think leaders hear that word and they say, "If I show vulnerability, my people will think I'm weak." The reality is the complete opposite. If you show vulnerability, you show that you are human. You invite compassion. You foster the collaboration you have so desperately been demanding for decades. You draw from that equity that you have been building up as a leader in your community—your internal community being your workplace culture, and your external community being the clients and the customers that you serve.

❝If you show vulnerability, you show that you are human. You invite compassion. You foster the collaboration you have so desperately been demanding for decades. You draw from that equity that you have been building up as a leader.❞

BB: It comes down to establishing trust and building trust. Those are two different things. This is the problem with most leaders. Being a leader can be extremely lonely, because you feel like, "Who can I talk to? Who can I confide in? Who's going to understand what I'm going through?" Most business owners find it very difficult to have conversations with your spouse about a lot of different things—unless you work together—because there isn't the context. Or employees, because there are certain conversations you just can't have. But it's really important for those conversations to build a cadre of like-minded people. I was on a call the other day. The conversation was about building CEO forums, leader forums, manager forums, where people can talk amongst themselves about the issues that they're having and say, "I'm scared. I don't know which way to go. I just laid off 500 people. Where do we go from here?" I guarantee you, there's going to be someone within that group of people who either has gone through a similar situation or has gone through something or knows somebody who's gone through a situation and knows a way out of the hole. There's a joke about two people at the bottom of a deep dark hole, with no idea how to get out. All of a sudden, somebody up top starts pouring water into the hole. "Listen, what are you doing?" He says, "I'm getting you out." "What? You're pouring water!" And he pours more and more water down the hole, and the water rises and lifts them to the top of the hole. That's a great lesson. There are people who have a different viewpoint, different experiences, different thought processes than you do. And the more we can lean on each other—and it doesn't just have to be other leaders; it's also leaning on the people within your company. There are people within your company—and I don't care who they are—who have brilliant ideas about how to move forward. They see things that you don't see. They're talking to customers that you're not talking to. They're talking to vendors that you're not talking to. They're looking at processes or they're looking at data that you're not looking at. And the more you can ask, "Who's got some ideas? Let's throw some things against the wall. No idea is a dumb idea." Let's talk to each other and come up with different ideas and be open to that. Let's say, "As a leader, I don't have to have every single answer to every single problem. I'm going to lean on the people I know, like and trust to help me work through this." Because we're so much stronger together. We have a far better view of what the current scenario is and where the future lies. That's where we need to be looking.

❝There are people within your company who have brilliant ideas about how to move forward.❞

CC: It's amazing what happens when a leader, a true leader, acknowledges that he or she does not have all the answers. What better excuse than a global crisis—one that is unprecedented in any time in history—to admit that you don't have all the answers? There's not one person on the planet who has all of this figured out. So if you've been waiting for an excuse, finally, to admit that you don't have all the answers, meet COVID-19. Something amazing does happen when you sit with employees who are closer to the processes, closer to the customers, closer to the data, closer to the real-world problems and opportunities that exist within your company, and you ask, "What would make your job simpler, easier, more effective, safer?" When you invite that granular of a conversation, you'll be amazed at the feedback you get. Again, when we were riding this wave of prosperity and there was little that you could do as a leader to screw that up, leaders stopped asking their employees for suggestions on how to be more efficient, effective or innovative. So workers stopped being as effective, stopped being as efficient, and certainly didn't raise their hand and say, "I've got this amazing idea, this breakthrough innovation that is going to vault our business into the next stratosphere." That's part of why we started these conversations. How can leaders look through this crisis—not overlook it, but look THROUGH this crisis—and say, "How can we leverage what we have, who we are, why we exist, to get through this crisis as a stronger, more unified, more competitive, and more sustainably successful business?" It's through leaning, and it's through learning.

❝What better excuse than a global crisis—one that is unprecedented in any time in history—to admit that you don't have all the answers?❞

BB: You talked about the fact that over the last number of years, leaders have just assumed, and moved forward with those false assumptions, which has led to record amounts of disengagement. I think it's *Inc. Magazine* that found that 70% of employees are disengaged at work. *Forbes* says if 50% of people were out there looking for work—and all these stats are pre-COVID-19, so take it in context—but that this was costing the US economy about half a trillion dollars a year. That every employee you lost cost you $100,000 to replace. Think about that. If you listen to your people, understand and value them— and the key words are listening, understanding, value— if we can do that, it's amazing the insights we're going to learn about our own company. Because everybody's been dashboarding everything. Everybody says, "The managers create a report that goes up to the director, that goes up to the VP, that goes up to the senior VP, that goes up to the C-Suite." Well, every single step along the way, that report has been whitewashed. And so, by the time the information gets to the CEO's or CFO's desk, it's a sanitized version of what the people who are actually seeing the issue actually said. If we can bypass that, and get back to a point where we're actually listening to our people and giving them the voice and allowing them to say things unfiltered, and say, "Hey, look, we have a problem here; if we don't pay attention to this, we're going to be in trouble." A lot of people are afraid to put that information forward as managers, because they don't want to speak truth to power. But if we don't do that, if we don't have a true pulse of what's going on in our company—and our people have a far better pulse of what's going on our company than we do—then we're going to lose insight and the ability to act, react and move forward. So I'm with you: We need to go back to having that internal communication and actually talk to each other, and stop dashboarding and stop assuming that analytics are absolute truth. Analytics and data are important, but data interpreted, communicated and understood is what we need. That comes through effective communication, both internally and externally.

❝If we don't have a true pulse of what's going on in our company... then we're going to lose insight and the ability to act, react and move forward.❞

CC: Boy, that journey you just took us through—from employee suggestion at the ground level, all the way to the ultimate decision-maker—was exhausting. But so true to life. Think about how diluted and inefficient that process has traditionally been. So now we're in crisis mode, and we don't have as many people on the ground or hierarchically as we did even a few months ago, because of the world in which we are operating currently. Think about how much more efficient businesses could be if the leaders go straight to that worker who is closest to the issue, challenge or opportunity, and say, "What do you need to make this better?" He tells you what he needs; you decide on the spot, "Yes, go and run with it" —

and just like that, you've implemented an innovation, a simpler process, a cheaper process. The fewer steps a process has to touch, the less time and money it's going to cost you. Just the simplification that a crisis of this magnitude forces companies to go through is such a lesson for leaders who are paying attention.

BB: And empowering those people to make decisions. That's the problem. It's that too many companies—especially as the companies get larger and larger—have lost the ability to empower their people to make decisions, to help their customers, to support their vendors, to make decisions that are going to impact a local group or small team of people. They can't even make a decision on something that's going to impact just their team, because it has to be run up the food chain. That's a problem that leads to so much inefficiency, so much bureaucracy, so much lag time, that it frustrates not only the people inside the company. So, therefore, you're right: They just don't care anymore. Frustrated employees just stop caring. The phrase I use is, "Your brand is only as strong as your unhappiest employee on their worst day." If your employees are unhappy in aggregate, what does that do to your brand? What does that do to your customers? How do your vendors, how does the world see you? How do they engage with you if, all of a sudden, every single time they're reached with an employee that just knows how to say no, and just follows this linear line without any interpretation whatsoever?

❝Your brand is only as strong as your unhappiest employee on their worst day.❞

CC: If in good times, on that wave of prosperity we keep referring to, there is a significant percentage of your workforce who are disengaged, who don't care, who have stopped innovating, who have stopped going above and beyond—who do "just enough not to get fired"—think about now. You're in times of crisis. Those same people, and those around them, are so distracted by and concerned about this pandemic, that what else gets sacrificed? Well, safety takes a huge hit. I don't care if you are an office-based business or primarily out in the field working around dangerous equipment: Safety gets sacrificed when people take their eye off the ball, and people take their eye off the ball if they are worried about anything beyond their job. You used such a key word earlier: "empower." When we simplify the decision-making process, and we empower people to make those decisions down the line—especially in times of crisis, when there is so much beyond our control and leaders are anxious, leaders feel like "Because I don't have all the answers, I'm feeling some anxiety too"—when you go farther down that hierarchy, think about your people, who have little to no control over how COVID-19 will impact their families, how the decisions of the leaders up the chain will impact their job, IF they're going to have a job either during the crisis or after, because the decisions of the leaders who don't take their opinions and feelings and contributions into account may in fact bury the business. So not only am I furloughed, but now I'm completely out of a job in the future. If you give them some empowerment—the core of that being "power"—to make decisions that will improve the job they do and the contribution they make, you've given them back some measure of control that the pandemic has taken away from them.

❝Safety gets sacrificed when people take their eye off the ball, and people take their eye off the ball if they are worried about anything beyond their job.❞

QUESTION:

Whom do you turn to when you don't know where to turn? Why?

_____

_____

_____

_____

_____

_____

_____

_____

_____

_____

EPISODE 3

CLARIFYING YOUR MISSION

BB: We've gone through an incredible change in our lives. I think most people need to realize that great things are going to come out of this. We will absolutely get through this. We need to ask, "Where are we going now?" The big issue we need to talk about next is mission clarity, which is huge. As far back as I can imagine, companies have created these lofty mission/vision/values statements that mean nothing. People go away on retreats—and I've been part of these retreats, I will admit it, and I am reformed—and built these mission/vision/values statements that are pithy statements with key words that speak to the values of the company. Then everybody goes "Rah rah rah," slaps themselves on the back and says how wonderful they are and how wonderful we are as a group, and then all this hard work gets forgotten. The pithy statements get posted on a wall somewhere, but they never get talked about. They never become part of the onboarding conversation. They're not part of the everyday conversation of how the company operates: Who are we as a company, what we do, why we do it, who we serve, what makes us valuable, where we came from, where we're going, what differentiates us in the minds of our customers, and why they care about us. We need to get rid of these mission/vision/values statements, because nobody remembers them and nobody lives them. We need to create a brand story instead. A brand story takes all the elements of the mission/vision/values statement, but it turns into a story. As a society—for 10,000, 20,000, 30,000 years, however long humans have been around—we've been telling stories. And we've been telling effective stories. Those stories get passed on from generation to generation, and they change and evolve, and the wording changes, and things happen, and people add and detract things. But the basic idea, tenets and values of that story remain the same. That's what we need to build within our companies. From the minute somebody is onboarded to the company until the day they leave and beyond, we need to ingrain every single employee with the brand story of the company and give each of them the power to internalize, recall and retell that story—not only internally, but also to vendors, friends, family and customers—because when it's lived, when people have the ability to make it their own and retell it in their own way, they internalize it. And then it becomes part of their mission, and it becomes what they can understand—why they matter to the company— because they are telling the story from their own internal point of view. And it engages them. It allows people to be retained and grow from the company. So, I wanted to get your thoughts on this, Claire.

❝Get rid of these mission/vision/values statements, because nobody remembers them and nobody lives them. We need to create a brand story instead.❞

CC: You're tapping into part of what enrages me about a lot of companies: You ask people what their company's mission is, and they immediately look around and say, "It's here somewhere.... Which wall is it on?" They equate MISSION with a mission statement. But those two things, in my mind, could not be more different. Your use of the word "story"—brand story, company's story—in place of the word "mission" is an important word change and emotional change. Because the word "mission," which is at the core of what I do with my clients, has been so misused. When I work with businesses and business leaders, that is always, always where we start: We get crystal-clear on their mission. Not "Can you recite the mission statement?" Because the answer is no; and even if you can, it's meaningless. I had this conversation with a business leader not too long ago, and I asked him that very question: "What's your company's mission?" His eyes rolled up to the top of his head, because he was trying to recall word for word what the mission statement was, as stated on their website. As with most of these global companies—very big, very successful—it was filled with a lot of highfalutin corporate words that were actually a load of crap. And, like you, I drank the Kool-Aid in the past, and I have been part of corporate communication groups, and I've been part of edicts to create mission statements. So, great, he recited or at least got the essence of it. Then I asked, "Do your people know what the mission is?" His answer was, "Well, they should." I said, "How do you know?" He responded, "Well, we go out all the time and do roadshows, and we repeat the mission, and we repeat the vision and the values. So unless they're living under a rock"—direct quote—"of course they know the mission." I said, "If you wouldn't mind, let me play that back for you the way I heard it. So, you go out..." "Yeah." "...and you report out..." "Yeah." "...and you communicate OUT the mission statement." "Yeah...." I asked, "What are you getting BACK from those people, to confirm that they get it?" Now, if you've ever met up with a deer on the road who gets stuck in your headlights, you know that glassy-eyed stare that they get, where they're not quite sure where they came from and where they're going. That was the glassy-eyed stare I got back. Because the reality is, a lot of businesses are really, really good at writing mission statements, or paying some glossy communications company to write it for them, and they're really good at formatting the document to make it look pretty. But a "pretty" mission is not a fulfillable mission. If it's not embedded in your culture, and it's not authentic to that culture and why you exist, it is a waste of money. So your use of that word "story," and getting people to understand that people need to find personal attachment to a company's mission, is key, because it's the mission in terms of their purpose. My WHY has to somehow be fed by the company's why. My role in your company has to show me how I am part of your story, and how I have some POWER—there's that word again— to impact that story, move it forward and make it better.

❝A "pretty" mission is not a fulfillable mission. If it's not embedded in your culture, and it's not authentic to that culture and why you exist, it is a waste of money.❞

BB: The key word is "internalize." Going back to your roadshow scenario, people go out and talk about things all the time. They talk about how great we are, this is what we do, this is why we do it, this how we do it—but they don't take the time to say, "Did people internalize this? Did they get it? Was it meaningful for them?" They miss gathering that engagement, reaction and feedback from the people they're trying to motivate, inspire and relate to. It's like any conversation: If somebody is just nattering at me, guess what? 90% of the time it goes in one ear and goes out the other. And if you ask me 15 minutes later what the person talked about, I might give you a few high points; if you ask me two days later, I probably give you nothing. But if we're having a conversation, and if it's back and forth, and you're asking questions, I'm asking questions, and we're clarifying, and we're able to put it in a position where everybody gets it and they're internalizing it, they can retell it. They can tell you what it means to them. That's when the magic occurs. That's how corporations are going to move forward from this point. You said in a previous episode that your brand story can't be about COVID-19. But it has to be part of it. It has to be, "We went through this together, and this is what we learned from it." It's important not to be defined by COVID-19, but you can't ignore it either. Your life and your business can't just be about the highlight reels; it has to be about the things that happened along the way that slammed you in the head, beat you up, and you were able to overcome. Because that's what people want. The brand stories, the heroes' journeys. Look at the Lion King, for example. It's not just "Simba was born; he became king; the end." It's all the trials and tribulations along the way that made him such a great king at the very end of the movie. That's what keeps us engaged, that's what keeps us believing in Simba, and that's what keeps us believing in leaders: to realize that they're human beings, they're going to make mistakes, they're going to have faults, and they're going to have missteps. But it's how they acknowledge it and say, "Hey, listen, we went this way, we thought it was going to work out great, and guess what? It didn't. But this is what we learned from it, and this is how we were able to regroup. This is what we were able to come out of this day, and this is how we're better because of it." Now THAT becomes part of your brand story. That's part of your mission, your vision, your values. It's saying that we're not perfect. The day a child realizes that mom and dad aren't perfect, it's earth-shattering. The sooner you can teach your kids that "I'm not a perfect human being and I'm going to make mistakes, but I'm going to work with you to try to make things better," you become a better parent. I think it's the same thing as a leader: When you can admit your faults—when you can say, "We made a misstep; we thought this was going to work out; well, it didn't, but these are the things that we were able to salvage from this, these were the things we learned from this, and these are the things that we were able to do because of it"—that gives people a reason to want to be part of it. Whether it's customers, employees, or vendors, that's a story that people can believe in. That's the story that people are going to retell. That's what we need to be thinking of in terms of our mission. Because if we can get our employees to tell that story, we can cut our marketing budget by two-thirds, because they'll tell that story, our customers will tell that story, and our vendors will tell that story. And suddenly we've got people flocking to us without paid advertising!

❝It's important not to be defined by COVID-19, but you can't ignore it either. Your life and your business can't just be about the highlight reels. People want the brand stories, the heroes' journeys.❞

CC: You are 100% right: Your employees are your best brand ambassadors, your best advocates for your story. I love that you brought up Simba—not just because the Lion King is a great movie and an even better musical—but the reason we loved him was because he was a flawed leader. He's the type of leader we truly follow—not the one who pretends that he's a superhero, or she has all the answers. It's the ones who can admit that they don't know all the answers, and that's why they've surrounded themselves with people like you and me who can help them get to the right solution, if we are properly empowered. If we think back to the first time, as children, we ever ran into one of our teachers in the grocery store.... I can remember one time I saw my pediatrician's nurse in a restaurant. When you're a child, the first time you see one of these authority figures out in the real world, walking the same streets you do, it isn't until that moment that you realize that they are human as well. But they must have food from time to time, and they need a dozen eggs and all of that. We start to see them not as this character with a role to play, but as an actual human who impacts our lives, and vice versa. So this notion that we all have a contribution to the story brings up for me this concept of impact. Impact should inform everyone's brand story as a company. What is our WHY? The why is not the widgets that we produce; it's the IMPACT that we have on the customer, the client, the community, the society we serve. Knowing and understanding that as a leader, we also have to understand "What is our impact?" The #1 driver of employee engagement is not my association with my individual job; it's my relationship with my direct manager. That is the biggest driver of engagement. And too many companies—and the larger ones especially fall victim to this—simply accept a wide variation in the ability of their managers to engage their people. We shouldn't stand for that. Because everyone has the capacity to empower, engage and accelerate the performance and the potential of the people who report to them. And the way you do that is through that power of why. It's why we are put in a position to lead in the first place, and it's why we are in the business that we are in, that should inform the mission and be the central plot of that brand story.

❝Everyone has the capacity to empower, engage and accelerate the performance and the potential of the people that report to them. And the way you do that is through that power of why.❞

BB: I agree. My biggest challenge with this is the Peter Principle: "People are promoted to their level of incompetency." Unfortunately, too many companies don't invest in their people; they do not give their people the mentoring, coaching and training to succeed as leaders. I'm a big believer of people first, then purpose, and then profit.

Purpose is your why—it's what you know, why do you do what you do—and I think that's really important. But the problem is, we're not investing in our people. We have too many managers, directors, vice presidents, senior vice presidents that we just promote because of the amount of time they've been in a company. But we don't give them the mentoring, coaching, training or soft skills they need to survive and thrive in the position. That's why we created our course, "Developing the Leader in YOU." It's all about the soft skills, the human skills of being a leader, that most people just never learn. They're just never taught because companies don't invest in their people, and they don't give them the ability to succeed. So you have people who have done a job, and now they're in a management position, and they don't know how to lead. Because doing the job is completely different from leading the people who are doing the job. It requires a different skill set, mentality and communication. That's really important for all of us to be thinking about: Moving forward, do we have the right people in place, leading our people, who are able to provide the mission/vision/values through brand stories, who are able to inspire our people to be the best and to get them to understand the true purpose of our company? Because if we don't, we're not going to survive and thrive through this, and we're not long term. Because management through authority, the carrot-and-stick style of management, is gone. There is a new paradigm, and it's all about understanding the people that you work with and inspiring them to be the best. Every leader—and I don't care if you're a frontline "manager" who manages five people to a senior vice president or a member of the C-Suite—needs to wake up every single morning and ask, "How can I help my people be better? What can I do to make things better for them?" Because we need to be thinking about that as leaders at all levels. How do we wake up every single morning and help our teams be better? If we don't, we're in trouble.

QUESTION:

Are your mission and vision still valid? If not, what has changed? How are you communicating your current or updated mission and vision so that others understand, embrace and believe in them—and convert them into meaningful brand stories?

_____

_____

_____

_____

_____

_____

_____

_____

EPISODE 4

THINKING BIGGER

BB: Even though we are currently in this pandemic, we are not going to be in here forever. It is up to leadership to ask, "Where are we now, where do we want to go, and what is keeping us from getting there?" Because as we come out of this pandemic, as we move forward, we need to be able to hit the ground running. If we're waiting for the world to open up and for governments to say we can start business again, we're going to be three to nine months behind the game. But if we're planning and organizing now, then when that day comes, our team will be ready, we'll be ready, our business will be ready, and we'll be the people others want to talk to, and we're already engaging our clients, getting them excited.

❝It is up to leadership to ask, "Where are we now, where do we want to go, and what is keeping us from getting there?"❞

CC: Ben, what a great way to tee this up. You set the context. And you hit the nail on the head. It feels like the world has gone asleep, that it's in hibernation. The most powerful, positive feature of this experience is the fact that, like no other time in any of our lives, this is a globally shared experience. Literally everyone we know—everyone in our family, everyone we do business with, everyone we encounter casually—is going through this same experience. Yes, from different perspectives, with different needs, and at different levels of anxiety or optimism. But it's a really powerful—inclusive, I dare to say—bonding experience. In the future, we'll ask one another, "Where were you in the spring of 2020? What was your life like?" Yes, we all have certain restrictions, but there are other things that we are learning. Any business, and especially any leader, who is sitting back and saying, "We're all in the same boat, in the same suspended animation, so I'm not going to put too much pressure on myself, my ability to lead my team, or our company's ability to look ahead, because everyone is being held back"—if that is a thought in your head, you've got to overcome that. And overcome that really, really soon. Because other businesses, other companies, other leaders are not letting this crisis hamper their ability to continue to do what they do, grow, pursue their mission, or refine their vision. So, while it is a globally shared experience, there's a unique opportunity for the right businesses and the right leaders to do something with this time, and not treat it as a pause button. Certainly it's a time for reflection, but if I had one stern warning for the universe out there, it's don't pause too long. Yes, reset, reassess and realign. But if you are not recalibrating while doing that, you're not going to emerge from this crisis healthy as a business. So that's a big caveat.

❝Don't pause too long. Yes, reset, reassess and realign. But if you are not recalibrating while doing that, you're not going to emerge from this crisis healthy as a business.❞

BB: Exactly. Like you, our business is across North America and worldwide. I'm dealing with a firm in Australia right now, and I'm really excited about what they want us to do for them. Their leadership contacted us—me and a partner in Australia—to do an engagement survey of a bunch of their customers, to ask, "What are the challenges you're facing right now?" So we're going to do these focus groups, these town hall meetings, with their clients to find out: "What are the challenges you're facing? What are the things that are keeping you from being successful? What are the things that you're afraid of?" We'll find out if there are ways that my company, my client, can help their clients succeed. We're going to do some engagement pieces, town halls, marketing, and a whole bunch of other things. But that's true leadership: It's realizing that by taking care of, communicating with and working with our customers, we're going to build that affiliation and loyalty. Yes, it may cost them more in the short term, but in the long term, the dividends will be there, because those clients are not going anywhere. They're going to say, "They took care of us, they listened to us, they understood us, they valued us through this whole crisis, and because of that we're going to be loyal to them moving forward." So I think that businesses need to be creative. It's not just saying, "Look at me," it's saying, "What can we do to make our clients' lives better?" and focus on that. Because as a leader, you may say, "You know what? What we're doing right now is not serving our clients. We may need to pivot." We may need to say, "We've got the brain trust, we've got the equipment, but we can look at things in a different way.

31

In Canada right now, and in the United States, a lot of breweries have refocused, and they're now making hand sanitizer! That's a brilliant thought process. Alcohol is the main ingredient of hand sanitizer, at 60-70%, so they're taking those tools and the expertise that they already have and turning around and making hand sanitizer. That's leadership. That's what we need to focus on: How can we pivot as companies, as leaders, as citizens to make this world better moving forward?

❝How can we pivot as companies, as leaders, as citizens to make this world better moving forward?❞

CC: It's such a great example. You often hear the term "victim mentality" used toward individuals who didn't have the best upbringing or had tragedy strike. You have two choices: You can play the victim and say, "The world is against me, and therefore I'm going to give up because I just can't catch a break." Or you can use those experiences as steps in your journey, and learning opportunities, and ways to pivot. We don't often use that phrase "victim mentality" with companies, but the breweries are such a phenomenal example of that creative pivot. In New Jersey, where I am, the microbreweries had been late arrivals in the state for a variety of reasons, but they were finally permitted to open up. And boy, they're everywhere now. But they're relatively small. They are just so passionate about brewing beer; and my husband and I are extremely passionate about patronizing their establishments. That is a business that had a golden opportunity to play the victim and say, "This is going to be our swan song; this is going to be the death knell for our industry or our business because we're just too small." But they have made this conscious choice to think bigger, rather than to play small. It's such a big pivot to go from playing small to thinking bigger, and then playing bigger. The distilleries and breweries in New Jersey and across the country said, "We can shut our doors, lay off everyone, and hope that we get out of this cave alive; or we can do something that gives back and keeps our business viable." It's such a phenomenal example of taking what could have turned them into victims of this crisis into an opportunity to ascend to a higher form of service delivery.

BB: We all need to be thinking that way. We all need to be rising up. I had a conversation with a client in Texas, who said, "The local market is depressed; there's nothing going on." I said, "Wait a second. You have a Zoom account, right?" "Yeah." "You have a website, right?" "Yeah." "You can still offer what you offer to people around the world. You are now a citizen of the world." The one thing that COVID-19 and this digital revolution, if we want to call that, is going to do is say, "I can now hire somebody from Texas if I live in New Jersey, or I can hire somebody from Amsterdam if I live in Australia." It's good to ask, "Who are the best talents? Who are absolutely the best talents? Who are the people I know, like and trust?" It doesn't matter if they're sitting side by side with me or they're half a world away: If they make it easy for me to do business with them, if they make it easy for me to be a customer, they understand me, they value me, they listen to me... why WOULDN'T I do business with them? It's the companies that ask, "How can I make it easy for people to do business with me? How can I take care of people? How can I make sure that it's people first, purpose second, profit third?"—those are the companies that are going to succeed. Now, we all need profit, there's no question we all need profit, this is not a communist society—I am a for-profit corporation and charge accordingly—but I truly believe that if we don't have purpose, if we don't take care of our people, and I'm talking internally and externally, we're missing the boat and we're going to be left behind.

CC: The word that comes up for me here is "connection." That is what it has always been about. When you talk to people about how they grow their business, how they gain new customers, how they get more sales, it's not about having the best product or the shiniest brochure. It's about how deeply I can connect to what you truly need, and how we can deliver a solution. That need to make a connection, which is so essential in business, has become even deeper and more critical in this pandemic. But I do think, because of the time that we live in, the technology—whether it's video conferences like we are on right now, or other technology that does make it relatively seamless to connect to someone between New Jersey and Canada, between Amsterdam and Australia, all of those examples—we really do live in an extraordinary time. We've never seen a pandemic like this; okay, I get it. But, again, I think what we are enabled to do, both through technology and just within ourselves, is to look at the situation creatively and say, "This will not stop me from serving my clients." If you look at it from the right perspective—it's the half-empty versus half-full, the victim mentality versus the service mentality—it really is a critical time, during this shared global experience, to step up your game, think in a different way, and serve on a bigger scale.

❝If you look at it from the right perspective... it really is a critical time... to step up your game, think in a different way, and serve on a bigger scale.❞

BB: It's true. I'll take it one step further. I don't think that the glass is either half-full or half-empty; it's refillable. If we look at the glass being refillable, the opportunities are amazing. The opportunities are absolutely amazing when you say, "Just because it's always been this way doesn't mean it always has to be that way; we need to move forward." For example, with technology, you and I are on Zoom—I'm in Vancouver, you're in New Jersey—and the world is watching us right now on YouTube. The fact that we can seamlessly integrate this technology and blast it out to anyone who wants to watch it worldwide is an incredible experience. They can watch it now or they can watch it later, and they can re-watch the material in it whenever and wherever they want. It's thinking as leaders with that mentality, asking, "What don't I know?" Because that's the thing: We don't know what we don't know. But the more we can ask questions, such as, "What am I not seeing? What don't I know? What are the opportunities that I'm just not seeing?" and talking to our people and listening to them and asking, "What are you seeing out in the market?" It's talking to our customers—"What are your pain points? What are you seeing? What are things that you'd like us to be able to help you with?"—that we're not currently doing.

Those conversations are going to lead to some incredible opportunities. It's a matter of leaders being able to synergize all that, develop a plan and a strategy, and then lead their teams forward to be able to be successful.

❝If we look at the glass being refillable, the opportunities are amazing.❞

CC: At the leadership level, at the company level—even at the entrepreneurial level, like you and I—we have become a community of learners. That had been enabled prior to COVID-19 by social media, by technology. Since I went from the corporate world into my own consulting business, nine years ago now, I have been amazed— pleasantly amazed—at the amount of openness and sharing in this network of entrepreneurs. Going in, I really thought it was going to be cutthroat and super-competitive. But because of the time we live in, and the world that we live in—which is growing in population, but shrinking in terms of ease of access and connection to each other—there are opportunities for literally everyone who chooses to see them. Some leaders were a bit slow to that concept, but they've learned that no one on the planet has the true answer or solution to this globally shared experience. There are a lot of people who were struck first, were caught flat-footed and had to react; there were others who saw it coming and started to prepare, but really didn't know what was going to stop the lava flow. We're still learning. But I think the more we foster transparency and learning, and admit that holding back knowledge and lessons learned is deadly to the entire global community—we can't overstate that enough— that translates into business, where leaders have this community of learning within their organizations. When I was in corporate HR, and running a training department, we were constantly asking, "How do we build a learning organization?" We struggled, as did other companies. I think we're almost there now as a result of the pivots that we have been forced into through this global pandemic. It's not just learning organizations anymore; it's learning communities. It's microcosms of teams, employees, leaders, companies and countries coming together to try to solve a universally felt problem through their unique perspectives. And I'm an eternal optimist. Which is not to say I've not had my share of hard knocks and all that. But I do try to look for, "What are those silver linings? What are the opportunities that come out of this? How can we learn, how can we be better, and how can we ensure that we don't repeat the sins of the past?" So this concept of a learning community—and this global realization that it took a global pandemic for us to finally get what that meant—boy, it's beautiful when you see it in action.

❝It's not just learning organizations anymore; it's learning communities. It's microcosms of teams, employees, leaders, companies and countries coming together to try to solve a universally felt problem through their unique perspectives.❞

BB: I think leadership is an attitude, not a job title. So when I say "leaders," I'm talking about managers who don't just manage processes, but actually lead and inspire people. Directors, vice presidents, executive vice presidents, CEOs: They're all leaders when they're inspiring people, building confidence and trust, and helping move the process forward. Those are leaders. But I think that leaders at every level need to find a cadre of people—and they might be within or outside your organization—that you can meet with within a cone of silence and say, "I just don't get this. We're wringing our hands, we're pulling out our hair, we just don't understand. We're frustrated by this." Maybe somebody within that group has already figured it out. Or at least collectively, as a group, you'll be able to come up with solutions. That's coaching; that's mentoring; that's creating the mindset that more minds are better than one, and putting aside ego and saying, "It's okay not to know. It's okay to be vulnerable. It's okay to be in a position where you don't have all the answers." I belong to this great group of 25 or 30 people who meet every week on Zoom, and there's expertise from every region. Everybody asks, "How can we make things better for everybody?" Everybody chimes in, listens and contributes, and the meeting is getting better and better. That's only because there's respect in the room to say, "None of us has all the answers. None of us has seen everything." Some of us have a little more gray hair than others, and have been through 9/11 and Y2K and 2008, into the 80s and the gas crisis, and everything in between—and some of us haven't—but it's that collective knowledge, and realizing that you never know where good ideas are going to come from. We all need to listen to each other and help each other to move forward.

❝That's creating the mindset that more minds are better than one, and putting aside ego and saying, "It's okay not to know. It's okay to be vulnerable. It's okay to be in a position where you don't have all the answers."❞

CC: I could not agree with you more. That is another positive outcome: This pandemic is forcing us to be more human in general. If ever there were a time to show vulnerability and to admit that you don't know everything, now is the time. This crisis that we're in removes the fear of saying, "I truly don't have an answer to this. I don't see the end of the tunnel. I don't know how to get us through this." I'm hopeful that this will teach all of us. Because I have been a victim of this as well. You're trained or groomed or raised to believe that if you say, as a leader, you don't know something, or you admit to a weakness or to vulnerability, that it's a sign of frailty or failure. But it's absolutely the opposite. And again, if this experience got people to develop muscles around showing vulnerability, expressing vulnerability, and laying it out there and saying, "I know you're vulnerable too. Let's not dwell on what you're vulnerable about. Let's work together to strengthen the community"—this has been the global lesson. And it's a very big business lesson as well to say, "It took a pandemic, but I finally said out loud that I'm scared, I don't have all the answers, I don't know that I'm going to be able to keep the doors open or keep all of my people, and I don't quite know what to do about it. And the sky didn't fall down on me when I said it."

It's amazing what happens when you finally admit what everybody around you already knew: You're not perfect.

❝It's amazing what happens when you finally admit what everybody around you already knew: You're not perfect.❞

BB: When you say, "I don't know," when you wring your hands and you throw your hands up, that does not lead to any trust; that doesn't inspire anybody. But when you say, "I don't know, but let's find out together," or "Let's build a task team to find out," or "Let's go find an expert who really does," as a leader, that inspires your team. That shows the vulnerability to say, "I don't know everything, but I'm going to go find out, take the time, make the effort, and invest the money to make sure that we have those answers." Because those answers need to be found out. And instead of "fake it til you make it"—which is just not going to work anymore—we need to be thinking, "I don't know, but I need to find out." It's not a sign of vulnerability; it's a sign that the world has had a monumental change for the better. Our children will be telling the story of COVID-19 to their grandchildren. That's reality. What 9/11 was for you and me—and we always remember where we were on 9/11—our kids will remember where they were in the spring of 2020 and be able to tell that to their grandkids. That's how much the world has shifted; this has been a tipping point in history. It doesn't matter if you're in Bangalore, India, or London, England, or Vancouver, BC, or New Jersey; we all had similar experiences. They were different—obviously New York, New Jersey had far more death and carnage than Vancouver did—but the shared experience of the fear and the unknown and the lack of leadership, and when you finally find leadership, we were apt to say, "They're doing their best and they're going to make mistakes and they're going to go down the wrong path, but they're going to admit that and they're going to and say, 'This is what we learned from this, this is how we're changing, and this is how we're going to move forward.'" I think that there are some great lessons learned. I think back to John McCain and Maple Leaf Foods—when people died because of a listeria infection—and he stood up day after day in front of the cameras and said, "This is what happened, this is what we're doing, this is what we're going to do." When fallible leaders take ownership and they own the situation, we respect them so much more, and we're willing to follow them much more easily.

❝When fallible leaders take ownership and they own the situation, we respect them so much more, and we're willing to follow them much more easily. ❞

CC: You're right: Some of us were far closer to the impact zone geographically and therefore emotionally. We recently marked the 25th anniversary of the Oklahoma City bombing. I remember exactly where I was when that news broke, even though I was in New Jersey then. Those tragedies, accidents, terroristic attacks—and it doesn't always have to be terrorism—these devastating tsunamis—any of that sort of trauma that is globally observed, even if it's not globally experienced, creates unity, the mentality that "We've got your back; we know what you're going through; we're in this together." As you were talking about McCain and other examples of pivots that have forced us to demonstrate vulnerability, it occurred to me that the greatest leaders I have ever known, or studied, or had the opportunity to work under, have a skill set that mediocre and other otherwise "marginally good" leaders don't. It's the same skill set that you and I have had to develop to survive as entrepreneurs, which is asking questions. It's not "skillful," because that sounds too manipulative; but asking good, deep questions. Because if you ask a run-of-the-mill leader, "What kinds of questions do you ask your people?" he or she is going to respond, "I don't ask, because I'm supposed to have the answers." No, you're not. If you were supposed to have all the answers, you wouldn't need staff. If you could do everything yourself, if you knew all the answers, if you knew how to run a business from every single angle—how to design, strategize, build and deploy it— you wouldn't need a team. It would be a hell of a lot easier to run a business if it was just you, and everything was within your control. But the reality is, you DO have a staff. You DO have a team. You DO have people to lead. Maybe they have knowledge that you do not. Woe to you if you don't tap into that. The best way to do that is to ask them. Sometimes it's incumbent upon a leader to say, "I don't know the answer to that, and I don't know how to go about finding that out. How do we figure out that solution?" It's amazing to me what happens—and I've seen it firsthand—when a leader goes to one of his people and asks, "How would you do this differently?" It is an amazing question that a lot of managers and leaders are afraid to ask, because they say, "Well, if I ask them that, I'm going to get a boatload of complaints and a boatload of things that are just not possible." I say to those people, "How do you know? Based on what experience?" Go ask them. They're already here, doing a job. But are they truly pouring their best talent, effort and thought into it? Or have they stopped innovating because you've stopped asking?

❝The greatest leaders I have ever known, or studied, or had the opportunity to work under have a skill set that mediocre and other otherwise "marginally good" leaders don't... which is asking questions.❞

BB: My favorite thing to do when I had staff was, if people had a problem, my door was always open, but you had to come in with two solutions: We could do X, or we could do Y. I may not take either, I might take a hybrid of them, or I might suggest that we augment one of them in a certain way. But at least it gave them the opportunity to know that I was empowering them to come up with a solution, that I was trying to make them better. Instead of being the all-wise guru on the hill, I would ask, "How would YOU handle this situation? You work here, you deal with these customers day in and day out, you know them far more intimately than I do. What would make things better for them?" When you empower your people to make those decisions and come up with solutions and develop their own form of leadership, your team is always going to be better. And that's what leaders should do: They should inspire their teams to be better. They should wake up every morning and ask, "What are the tools my people need to be more effective today?" That's where leadership needs to go. As leaders moving forward, I agree with you: We can't know everything, we can't do everything, we can't be everywhere. So we need to empower our people. Command and control, carrot-and-stick—gone. Forget about it. It's done. There's too much information on the information superhighway. They just have to go to GlassDoor or Yelp and they're going to know that, "Wait a second, we're not being treated as well as the company down the street. Why should I be working here when I can go work there? If I'm not being treated fairly, if I'm not being valued, if I'm not being empowered, why would I not walk out the door and go somewhere else?" Every person you lose costs you a hundred thousand dollars to replace. Be a leader.

CC: What's funny is, partly because of the stay-at-home restrictions, I recently rediscovered my love for the show, The West Wing. First of all, it is as relevant now as it was 20 years ago, when the series first aired. But when I watch those episodes, and I watch Martin Sheen as the President—yes, it's partly idealized, and obviously everything's scripted—it's an amazing illustration of leadership. This is a character who has a doctorate in economics—he's a highly educated, really smart guy who knows his stuff—but you'll notice that he never makes decisions on his own. He surrounds himself with the best and the brightest who can advise him. Every time he takes a meeting in the Oval Office, some combination of his inner circle and other advisors, the Joint Chiefs of Staff, etc., come to him prepared with information and say, "Here are the facts, based on my expertise and my role and the accountability that you have instilled in me, and this is what I recommend we do." He takes all of that in, and he makes as informed of a decision as possible. If it's the right one, it's great and he shares the credit; if it's the WRONG one, the buck stops with him. It drives home this point that somebody who is supposedly the most powerful person in the world—at least that's what Americans have had the world believe—his decisions are only as good as the information he takes in, processes and acts upon. But he is the first to admit that he is not an army of one; he is not a team of one. He is the figurehead, the spokesperson, but it is all based on, "What do the people around me suggest? What do they know? What did they research? What do they stand behind? NOW I'm going to make a decision, because I don't have all the answers." If the President can say, "I don't have all the answers, and I'm not just going to go in front of a microphone and make it up"—and I'm still talking about the West Wing character—then who among us as leaders would be arrogant enough to say, "I don't need to ask anyone any questions; I don't need to admit to what I don't know"? That's not what a leader does.

BB: Let's take that one step further, because I am a West Wing junkie too! Let's talk about Ainsley Hayes. Ainsley Hayes was a long-legged blonde, gorgeous, Republican lawyer from Atlanta—I believe from Atlanta, Georgia—and totally contrarian to the Democratic agenda, totally contrarian to the viewpoints of a lot of the staffers and the senior staff of the people within the West Wing. But Jed Bartlet, President Bartlet, hired her anyway, because he said he liked to have smart people around him. He said, "She's smart people, and she's going to give me a voice and an attitude and a thought process that nobody else in my administration was going to give me." She ended up being a powerful character, because she was that contrarian voice of reason. She didn't say, "You say this, so I'm going to say that." She would say, "I serve at the power of the President, and I'm loyal to the President and to the philosophy of the Presidency, but I'm going to look at things from my Republican roots, not just drink the Democratic Kool-Aid." So, it's having leaders bring people around them who may be contradictory to their particular viewpoints, who may believe different things than they do, and have the skillset to back up their convictions. If you can be constructive, and you can have those conversations with these people who believe things that you would never believe, you're going to be far more insightful and have a far more global viewpoint than if you're just insular and surround yourself only with people who believe exactly what you believe and say exactly what you say.

CC: Groupthink is the absolute death knell of a growing, innovative, competitive company. There's no question. Bartlet's choice to go out and get her on the team, no matter what objections she raised, was such a great example of a leadership style that said, "I'm going to create an environment where sometimes I'm going to yell and scream, because I so passionately believe in my position or what I want to do, but where you can come back at me if you passionately believe a different position. I don't think there's an episode where Jed Bartlet isn't having "a West Wing moment" and yelling. But it's such a well-done show, with well-drawn characters. The analogy or metaphor of that for modern-day leadership, of surrounding yourself with people who are strong-willed, have opinions, will share them and report to somebody who says, "Not only should you share them, if you sit quietly and you don't step up and speak up..."

BB: "...you're of no use to me."

CC: That's correct.

BB: And I think that is the leadership culture that we need moving forward. It's that good ideas can come from anywhere. I'm going to listen to all opinions. Ultimately the buck stops here, I'm going to make the decision, I'm going to gather as much information as I can, and I'm going to make as intelligent a decision as I can moving forward based on the information that's put in front of me, but I'm not going to ignore a piece of information just because it doesn't meet with my particular agenda. I think that great leaders now and moving forward need to have that philosophy in order to be successful. Because as you said, "groupthink," or having that whole silo mentality—it's looking at things in a way where it just doesn't make any sense. Here's a perfect example: 24, 25 years ago, I worked for Kinkos Corporate. My job was to handle all the corporate accounts in Western British Columbia. And once a year, Kinkos brought 800 salespeople and 800 operations managers to a central location for a three- or four-day conference. Sometimes we were all together, and sometimes the salespeople were in one room and the ops folks were in another. This was a particular time where we had 800 people in a huge ballroom with a dividing wall down the center, and the salespeople were in the room to the right, and the ops team was in the room to the left. On the sales side, we heard, "Value, sell value, build relationships, trust," all the things that go along with sales. Halfway through the presentation I went to the bathroom, and on the way back I thought to myself, "Just for interest, I'm going to sit in on the managers' conversation and see what's going on." Well, from their point of view, the message was, "Hammer them on costs, reduce costs." It was a completely different mindset, a different culture, within the same organization. No wonder the sales and ops teams within the organization hated each other. Because we were being compensated differently, the culture we were being indoctrinated into was different, the way we should treat customers was different, the way we should treat staff was different. And because of that, there was this huge dichotomy, this huge rift, and the organization obviously split apart because Kinkos ended up being bought out by FedEx, and I'm not even sure it exists anymore. But organizations need to have one central voice: "This is our culture, this is who we are, this is our purpose, this is how we treat our people." Because you have one job as an organization, and it's to take care of the customer. And when organizations and leaders focus their people on serving the needs of the customer, that's when success will really happen. When they're focused on "My team is bigger than your team, and my budget is bigger than your budget, and my department's more important than your department," the customer loses, and eventually the company loses.

❝That is the leadership culture that we need moving forward. It's that good ideas can come from anywhere.❞

CC: The siloed thinking, the siloed mentality, the siloed management of companies does not happen overnight. No one I know, who has built a business, started by putting pillars in the ground with big columns and saying, "We're going to pour finance into this one and this division into that one, and don't ever rise up unless you just need a drink of water—but other than that, don't consort with those people." Silos happen over time. One of the main reasons siloed management happens is that companies lose sight of the horizon. It creeps up on them, because suddenly they're reporting their results quarterly, monthly, whatever, and then they get enamored with, "We didn't make as much of a profit as we wanted to," or "We lost a top performer," or "Customer complaints are rising, so we're going to look at those lagging indicators, figure out whose fault it is, and put a Band-Aid on the problem." These are companies that have lost sight of the horizon they're trying to reach, if they ever had one in the first place. You talk about the culture, about "We're going to have one voice" and one philosophy around who we serve and how we serve them. Simon Sinek is dead-on right about this: You have to start with the why. Where are we heading? Why are we even endeavoring to do this? And the more clearly you can see the horizon as a leader, and the more clearly you can express that to your people in such a way that it resonates for them and their own internal guidance system, the stronger your culture will be, because you built it around that horizon, your why. It makes decisions a hell of a lot easier, because they are no longer about, "Is that going to fix the financial gap that we had last quarter?" Now they are based on, "Does this move us closer to where we said we wanted to be, and why we are in existence in the first place?"

❝One of the main reasons siloed management happens is that companies lose sight of the horizon.❞

BB: Organizations need to reevaluate their culture on a regular basis. They need to say, "What are the things that are keeping our culture from succeeding? Who are the people who are keeping our company from succeeding? What are the processes, the procedures, the dynamics that are keeping our people from succeeding?" A lot of it has to do with how you hire people, how you onboard people, the brand story you tell people. We'll get into the brand story in a different episode, because I think that's a conversation on its own. But we need to stop thinking about mission, vision and value statements as a nice-to-have, and something that has to be ingrained in every single person and has to be lived on a daily basis. With that I think you're going to be able to break down silos, build a stronger culture, and create opportunities for organizations to stop focusing internally and pointing fingers internally and saying, "It's their fault." Marketing hates ops, and ops hates marketing, and they both hate sales. The question is why? What's broken? What's creating the communication rifts that are causing this? What are the procedural things that are happening within the organization that are causing this animosity, causing this mistrust, causing things not to run as smoothly as they should? That's the leader's responsibility. Your responsibility is not to sit in your office, in front of your computer all day, and analyze charts. Your job is to ask, "What are the factors that are keeping our people from being the best that they can be and treating the customers the best that they can?" If that means sitting in on the customer service calls, sitting in a marketing meeting, going out on sales calls with salespeople, actually going to trade shows and standing on the show floor and having conversations with actual clients, that's what true leaders should do.

❝What are the things that are keeping our culture from succeeding? Who are the people that are keeping our company from succeeding? What are the processes, the procedures, the dynamics that are keeping our people from succeeding?❞

CC: The four or five questions that you just asked, the way you asked them in the beginning, then added to them with some more really good ones…. Any leader who says, "Well, I'm not good at asking questions; I wouldn't know the right questions to ask," put those on a Post-It note, put them in your pocket, and walk around and ask those very questions. Don't just bring your leadership team out of their silos—although that is a great first step, to get them out of their silos and really dig into those questions— but have those people, those leaders, walk around. I'm a big advocate of having walk-around questions for leaders. I work with a lot of leaders to equip them with that. They're not all cookie-cutter; but there are some powerful ones that are universally applicable, and you nailed those. So take those four or five questions, put them on an index card, and keep them in your pocket. Because they are going to open dialogue in a way that is going to remove barriers, increase collaboration, and turn on the innovation that so many companies have stepped away from.

BB: Thank you. Certain things just riff off your head.

CC: Well, you added to them and then tied in the "What are we doing that is causing this mistrust?" Those are important things to analyze as well. But the way that you phrased the beginning ones, they were more open-ended and hopeful in terms of tapping into the creative juices of the employees. Because they have that creativity, and they want to tell you how you can do a better job leading them. If you focus them on how we as a business can better serve the clients and customers we were put on this earth to serve, through this business, that's going to tell leaders how to lead them. Because if they can consolidate and unify around that vision—in a way that is built up organically and in a way that every person on the team can embrace, relate to, and see how they contribute—there's really nothing a company cannot accomplish.

BB: To further that, there's no one way to lead. There are ways NOT to lead, but there is no one way to lead. And you really need to have the pulse of your organization. Understand who are the people within your organization. What do they need? What employee X needs is not what employee Y needs, and Division X may not look at things the same way as Division Y. Head office versus branch

52

offices, office employees versus home employees. We need to look at this thing as not a cookie cutter, but as a way of saying, "These are human beings. Each human being has his or her own thoughts, needs, desires, fears. How do we relate to them?" A great leader equips the leadership at all levels to be able to lead their teams because, as we said at the very beginning, you can't do it all, you can't be everywhere, you can't do everything. So great leaders provide their people, the next generation of leaders, with the tool set that they need to become better leaders. My mindset, my mantra, is to allow us to develop the leader in you and create the opportunities where we can develop the leader in you at all levels. Because we need to learn how to lead. Yes, there are innate leaders; yes, there are people out there who are naturally more inclined to lead than others. But even those people who are naturally inclined leaders can always become better leaders. We can always be better. We can always be saying, "I did that really well. How could I have done it better?" It's not beating yourself up; it's looking for opportunities to say, "That was great, that was awesome, we had a great meeting, we did really, really well this quarter. That's phenomenal. Let's celebrate it. But what could we have done better?" and "How do we take this to the next level?" and "How do we make people even more excited?" That's how companies elevate: by celebrating the wins, but also by taking a look at the failures and saying, "Those are cool too. Those failures allowed us to be better moving forward." So let's not point fingers and blame people; let's say, "What did we learn from this?"

CC: You learn more from your failures than you do from your successes. A lot of companies have—again, this doesn't happen from the outset, but over time it creeps in—this culture of either blaming or putting the failures behind them as quickly as possible. Take the time to say, "Yes, it is absolutely important to celebrate the victories and give recognition to that." But it is equally important to get together, not in a blaming way, but to say, "We just had a failure. Cool. You know why that's a GOOD thing? Because those are our greatest opportunities to learn and to get better. So let's get together and pick apart how that failed, what we're going to learn from that, and what we're going to do better next time."

BB: Because you're pushing the envelope.

CC: Too many of these companies shove it under the rug. Leaders are not perfect. Jed Bartlet was not a perfect president. He did not make every decision flawlessly, even armed with the best information from the greatest minds he could surround himself with. There were still things in every episode that didn't go smoothly, that didn't go right. It's a matter of not hiding from that, but acknowledging, "We're not going to get everything perfect. But what we ARE going to do is keep our eyes on the horizon and lean into—not create opportunities for failure, but lean into—those times when we have fallen short and ask, 'What did we learn from this, and how do we come back stronger?'" A lot of companies talk a real good game about having a high tolerance for failure. I have not come across many companies who advertise and brag about that, but actually walk that talk. And it's hugely important to the growth and innovation of a company.

BB: If you're saying one thing and doing another, think about how that's frustrating the people inside your organization. How it's demotivating them. How much they become disengaged. How much less they care about your organization if you're constantly saying one thing and, when the rubber meets the road, you say, "We celebrate failures and we work together and we build these things together," and then all of a sudden the finger comes out and it points at you and says, "It's your fault." That's demoralizing. People around that person think, "If the finger's pointing at them today, could it be me tomorrow?" And it's not just that one person who becomes demoralized; it's not that one person who becomes disengaged. It could be a whole department. Or it could be a division. Or it could be the entire company. Because people talk. As organizations, we need to say, "This is who we truly are. This is what we're really about. This is what we're willing to stand for, and this is what we're willing to fight against. This is how we're going to live our lives day in and day out. We're not going to be perfect, we're going to make mistakes, and we're going to learn from them and move on. But these are the goals, and these are the things that we want to have the company built on." If you can actually do these things and create a culture that you can actually live and actually succeed in doing, it may not be a lot of things, but if you can do those things well, the great minds will flock to work for you.

CC: There's good news and bad news in that story. The bad news is when there is a conflict between what you say as a leader and what you actually do—what we advertise as our culture, and what the culture in fact is—it is human nature to follow the action, not the words. To dismiss the words if they conflict with the action. The common saying lately, at least in the States is, "Don't listen to what he says; watch what he does." That goes for any leader. The good news is—as much as it is in our human nature to, when in conflict, dismiss the words and follow the actions—it is also human nature to want to solve problems. If you present something to your employees as, "This is a collective problem that we all share, and it's holding back our ability to grow or, by extension, our employees' ability to advance and learn, but it's a problem we know we can solve"—that's going to tap into their human nature to step up their game, be creative, figure out a way around it, and work with the people around them to do exactly that. Companies that tap into their employees' innate ability and desire to solve problems get farther ahead. And what better time than during this self-imposed restricted mode? This is an opportunity for self-study. This is an opportunity for pruning what does not work—pruning what does not serve your company, your clients, and the people you employ—and getting stronger. Because I guarantee you, your competitors are doing exactly that.

"Companies that tap into their employees' innate ability and desire to solve problems get farther ahead."

QUESTION:

Do you find yourself thinking too small? What are you doing to create the opportunities that will lead to your definition of success?

_____

_____

_____

_____

_____

_____

_____

_____

_____

EPISODE 5

BUILDING FOR THE LONG TERM

CC: The NFL Draft took place this Spring. Over the years it has evolved into this almost Las Vegas spectacle—in fact, I think this year it was supposed to be in Vegas—and so everyone got creative and held the Draft remotely, and were responsible in terms of social distancing and all of that. But it occurs to me that all the professional sports organizations are in the same boat as any other business: They're not sure if their season is going to be postponed, shortened, changed to the point where teams are playing in front of virtual audiences instead of live audiences. I'm not concerned that the NFL as an organization is going to run out of money, but I think the fact that the Draft went on anyway serves as a good example for businesses. Because they don't know when the season will start, they don't know what changes will need to happen in this new world of ours. But they acted "as if"; they continued to lead "as if." If they had said, "We'll wait and see, and then we will adjust the Draft accordingly," they would have been behind the curve. Instead, they said, "It doesn't matter if our season is postponed, shortened, changed, etc. What doesn't change is our mission. And our mission is to win the Super Bowl." Every single team's mission is to win the Super Bowl. So how do we go about this Draft the way we would have gone about it had there not been a COVID-19 crisis? How do we build the best team, surround them with the best coaches who have the best chemistry to collaborate effectively—to command performance on the field and discipline in the locker room—and put together a strategy that positions us best to win the Super Bowl? It's a great example for all business leaders that the show must go on, albeit in a modified form, because we must remain focused on the mission.

BB: It's about understanding what your long-term purpose is. What is your long-term goal? What are you trying to achieve? There are so many businesses—I'm hearing this every day—saying, "We'll see where we are within 60 days. Call us in 60 days, call us in 90 days, call us in 120 days." Instead of saying, "In 60/90/120 days, the world is going to open up again." Eventually it's going to happen: We're going to go back to business. Business is not going to be normal—it's going to change; we're going to have to do different things—we all understand that. But it's the businesses that are saying, "You know what? It's quiet now. Why don't we jump on a call for an hour or two? Why don't we get the team together on a Zoom chat and talk about what we'll do, how we'll implement, how we'll move forward once everything opens up?" Because it's not like the economy is just going to flip a switch and then all of a sudden people are going to say, "Nobody was working, now everybody's working. Go!" It's just not going to happen that way. There's going to be a gradual shift. People are going to have to ramp up. Different industries are going to be relying on each other.

So everybody has to get in line and ready their supply chain, so they can be ready. The more we can be talking about that, the more we can be looking at "What's next? What do we need to do?" we need to make sure that, while it may not be business as normal, we're planning for the future, we're planning for the eventualities that this will go on and life will go on. I think that's really an important place to talk about today for business and leadership.

CC: No question. To your point, the biggest change that this has brought about is not around the "why" of a business; a lot of businesses need to heed that message, that their why is still a point on the horizon that they need to focus on. What has fundamentally changed, and has been impacted by COVID-19, is the HOW. Every client that I talk to, every business that I interact with, they all have said the same thing: "We took a hit, or we're challenged by cash flow right now, and that's a short-term issue. But on the bright side, what this has forced us to do is get very efficient. We have figured out that we can get our work done without a lot of the steps that we thought were necessary, and now we've concluded they were extraneous." And to your point about ramping up in a way that is logical, in a way that is strategic, in a way that is methodical versus haphazard, it's the HOW that is really taking the biggest impact. Where things have slowed down and things are a bit quieter, that should be a main focus of businesses: "We know where we want to get to long term. There are certain strategies we had developed prior to these forces that have acted upon us. What about the 'how' should we alter, augment or enhance? Let's focus on that right now, because the why is still where we should be headed."

❝What has fundamentally changed, and has been impacted by COVID-19, is the HOW.❞

BB: I agree. I look at the whole crisis as almost like my "normal" July and August. In July and August, usually very little happens: Everybody goes away on vacation, everybody's mindset changes, everybody wants to be on the golf course or on the tennis court or at the beach. Very few people want to be thinking about business. But I find that the leaders who actually take the time at that point—time to actually have those lunches, to have those meetings, to do the strategy—to figure out where they're going to be so when September 1 rolls around, or after Labor Day, they're ready. They're hitting the ground running. The inventory's in house, the people are in place, the training's been done, the efficiencies are there. They're ready to go. So when everybody else is thinking about, "Oh, wait a second, I gotta start thinking about work again," they're not spending the next six or eight weeks trying to ramp up; they're already ramped up and ready to go. And to your point, now is the time to be looking at policies, procedures, personnel, purpose— all the things that drive your business—and say, "Are we as effective as we could be?" Is there extraneous stuff, stuff that you're looking at like, "Why do we do this? Why are we actually continuing to do this? Maybe there's a more effective way, a better way, a more efficient way, even a more cost-effective way of doing things. Now is a time when we actually have some time; we can actually breathe and take the time to evaluate." Because if we keep doing what we've always done, we're going to be in trouble. It's not going to work. What we've always done in the past, what we did up to December 31, 2019, is not going to work on September 1, 2020. It's just not going to work. Your marketing has to change, your philosophy has to change, the way you evaluate, the way you interact with your customers—everything is going to change. It may only be slightly—it may just be a slight shift to the left or a slight shift to the right—but it's going to change. We all need to be asking, "How has our world been impacted?" and "What do we need to do to put ourselves in the best position to move forward?" I'm with you 100%.

❝Now is the time to be looking at policies, procedures, personnel, purpose—all the things that drive your business—and say, "Are we as effective as we could be?"❞

CC: You used the phrase, "If we do what we've always done." Normally the end of that sentence is, "We will get what we've always gotten." That's out the window. Because if we go back to the old normal, that place is gone. That way to interact with your marketplace and your employees and your customers and your prospective customers? That ground has permanently shifted. So the end of that sentence has to change now. How do we make sure that—when the doors open up again, and there are no barriers to interaction—how can we put things in place today, and strip out the extraneous, so that our people hit the ground running? I'm reminded that we ask ourselves that same question when we onboard new people: "How do we flatten their curve toward full productivity?" It's interesting that that phrase, "flatten the curve," has taken on new meaning, when we're talking about the curve of the impact of the virus. But that's really what we're talking about. Businesses—smart businesses, who still have one eye on the horizon, are staying mindful of their why, and are critically looking at the how—really need to undertake a systematic, enterprise-wide re-onboarding of their entire organization. Because it's not just going to be, "Okay, everybody, back to where you were." There's no going back. It's now, "In preparation for the doors opening up, this is what we will be about. The why has not changed; the how has changed. And here's what we're doing about it."

❝Smart businesses... need to undertake a systematic, enterprise-wide re-onboarding of their entire organization.❞

BB: It's interesting that you talk about onboarding, because I was just listening to a podcast over the weekend that had Grant Cardone on the show. He was talking about failure. He was asked, "What's one of your most recent failures?" He said, "We brought on 45 or 50 new people in January and had to let 42 of them go. The biggest reason we had to let them go is we had no way to onboard them. We had no way to bring them into the culture. We had no way to get them acclimatized to what we do, how we do it, our purpose, our values, and bring them into the organization properly, because we didn't have a way to bring them together. And it was unfair to try to do this remotely, over Zoom. They just couldn't get part of the culture." So they wanted to say, "Look, when this thing is over, we want to have you back, we absolutely do, but we just can't bring you on board successfully now." So they had to let these people go. Because they realized that they couldn't support them from an onboarding point of view. I found that fascinating. But you're right: We are going to have to re-onboard every single employee, because we're going to have to evaluate "Has our purpose changed? Has our vision changed? Have our mission and vision and values changed? Has the direction that we're going as a company changed? Has what we do changed? Has how we engage with our customers changed? Has how we communicate with our customers changed?" And if to any of those things the answer is yes, we need to take our employees back to Ground Zero and say, "This is where we were, this is now where we are, and this is where we're going," and be able to bring them back into this understanding that this is the new brand story. "Here's the light at the end of the tunnel, here's the hill that we're going to climb over, but where we were six months ago versus where we are today has fundamentally changed, and you all need to understand that." Because if they don't understand that, employees are going to revert to, "We always did it this way." That's not going to work anymore. So that's going to take effective communication, effective leadership, and better vision—understanding what is different about your company and being able to articulate it effectively, both internally and externally.

❝That's going to take effective communication, effective leadership, and better vision— understanding what is different about your company and being able to articulate it effectively, both internally and externally.❞

CC: Agreed. What a great opportunity for business leaders who choose to see it that way. The ones who are going to be at the forefront—not just competitively in the market, but truly as employers of choice—are going to be those leaders who do everything you just said, and paint the picture of the new normal: "Maybe the 'why' hasn't changed, but we got away from that because we became so good at firefighting." Now COVID-19 is the ultimate sweeping forest fire; it's the towering inferno. But we need to bring the "why" back into focus. Leaders have a critical opportunity to say, "This is who we are going to be now." Their employees are starving for that. They want to know that you're going to take care of them during this time of crisis, but they also want to know that you have your act together and have a plan for the longer term. Because a lot of people are already out of a job, a lot of others may follow suit, and employees don't want to just stay employed; they want to stay inspired. They want to feel like what they do matters. So employees are watching, listening, and seeing how their leaders are stepping up with a unifying vision of "This is how we collectively will get through this, and this is who we will become in the future."

❝Employees don't want to just stay employed; they want to stay inspired. They want to feel like what they do matters.❞

BB: That's going to be the difference between being able to hire and rehire great talent, and being the company that's starving for talent. Because, as you said, employees are now looking and saying, "I want to align myself with a company with purpose. I want a company that I believe is going to survive the next three to five years. I want to be with someone where I think that I'm going to matter, and I can believe in what their vision is and what they're going to be doing." If you can't articulate that as a company, if you can't articulate how you've changed, where your value is, and what your mission and vision are, you won't be able to bring onboard the talent that you need in order to get you there. And all of a sudden, even if you were a successful company, you're going to become a commodity very quickly. Because without the right people, that sense of purpose, and leaders who can communicate that purpose—and I'm not just talking vice presidents and CEOs, I'm talking all the way down to the team leaders at the ground level—everybody needs to be drinking the Kool-Aid and understanding the direction and where we're moving forward. Because if you don't have that, why does somebody want to jump on board? Why would somebody want to get a ticket on the Titanic, knowing that they're going to hit the iceberg? People are going to see your company as that iceberg out there.

CC: What's interesting is the example of Grant Cardone hiring 40 to 50 people in January, only to have to turn around and lay off the majority of them. The positions, the focus of roles, is changing as well. I was having a conversation with one of my clients recently, and she was looking to bring somebody else onto her team. It's a very functional, black-and-white accounting type of a role. What's interesting is we've shifted the focus from the need to fill a job description to "These are the competencies and the X Factor and the qualities that we need to look for"—not the least of which is an ability to learn and pick up things quickly and have an aptitude toward accounting or finance. But the traditional job descriptions? The progressive companies are throwing them out and saying, "We're going to figure out the best division of our labor, and who's going to do what, AFTER we figure out the right person to bring on the team." The right person with the right intangibles: that resilience that we've talked about, the ability to adapt, the ability to work in ambiguity, the ability to switch gears and go from showing up at an office 9:00 to 5:00, to working from home and still being able to produce with autonomy. Using the analogy of the NFL Draft, it's not just about hiring position players anymore; it's about hiring special teams. It's about hiring people—and I don't mean to beat that analogy to death—who can go on offense OR defense, who have enough of a flexible learning mentality that they can say, "It's less important to me what to-do list you assign me; it is more important that I believe in you as a company, I believe in where you're going, and in turn you believe enough in me to do everything you can to support my success."

BB: Being able to have the right people on board, doing the right things in the right way, is a huge differentiator, and will be for years to come.

QUESTION:

How are you evaluating the inefficiencies within your business, whether they relate to people, purpose, process or product? What changes will you make to become more effective and valuable?

_____

_____

_____

_____

_____

_____

_____

_____

_____

_____

EPISODE 6

BUILDING TEAMS AROUND THE INTANGIBLES

BB: We finished our last episode talking about personnel. I think that's a great place to start. We need to talk about building teams around the intangibles, because there are so many intangibles now in business. There are so many unknowns. There are so many reasons to pivot, shift or change. Hiring somebody who can just code in language X for this particular project is not a great idea anymore. We need to start looking at people as, "How are they going to fit into our organization, and how do they grow with our organization?" That's something that leaders really need to be thinking about moving forward.

CC: No question. This is another one that goes on the list of must-haves, which companies have talked a good game around for years and years, and have now become a "We have no choice but to move in this direction" scenario. Several months ago, I posted a rant on YouTube about job descriptions, and how rigid they tend to be in most companies. Every single company says, "We've got to get control of our job descriptions." No matter the size of the company, the number of distinctly unique job descriptions that it has is usually whatever that total population is, minus about two. Because everyone just takes the last version and modifies it. It's because we want geniuses who get along with everyone, know their place, know what's expected of them without you having to communicate with them, and are absolute show ponies. But the reality is, we're not employing robots; we're not employing machines. We're employing humans. And humans, by nature, are extremely unpredictable. But they're also highly versatile. So during my video rant, I said, "We're living in an age where genders are fluid; why can't job descriptions be fluid?" It's one of those holdovers from the Industrial Age, where you just put somebody in a box, you forget the resume that attracted you to hire them in the first place—because of all these other intangibles they brought to the interview, to their background—you put that in the drawer, hand them a job description, and say, "Don't color outside of the lines." So now, this isn't just an opportunity for leaders; it's a mandate to go away from those job descriptions and say, "We're going to start over and truly practice what we've been preaching for years, which is: We are going to hire based on culture, and then train based on skill."

BB: When I first started in sales 25, 30 years ago, a veteran salesperson came up to me and said, "Sales is sales, and product knowledge is two weeks." Yes, you absolutely need to understand what the company does. But it's the process—the ability to think, communicate, and be engaging, interactive and reactive—that makes a great salesperson. You need to take that great salesperson and ingrain him with your own culture. And that's with everybody: You have to take people's innate skills, their innate abilities, and say, "How can we make this work within our culture?" Because everybody says, "You're hiring for a position." You know what? Better to hire somebody about whom you can say, "We want this person to grow with the company." A generation ago, people stayed with companies 35, 40 years. I used to have one of the major airlines as a client, and the amount of people who wore 35-year-plus pins in that organization was astounding. You can still see it in some of the heavy manufacturing industries, but very few people say, "I joined the company at 18 and came out as vice president at the end of 35 years. I grew with the company, and they trained, mentored and coached me, and they brought me up through the ranks. They enabled me to become more than I actually thought I could be." I think we need to go back to that. We need to look at the human being: Will this person think for himself? Is she reactive? Is she personable? Is he a problem solver? What is his innate personality? Is it something that you can work with within your organization and say, "We're going to start this person in the mailroom. We're going to start this person at the front desk. We're going to start this person in a junior position. But we know that we want to keep this person; we know that we want to have this person around for a long time." So it's a matter of having those conversations, to say, "What are your aspirations? What are your goals? What would you like to learn? What are the things that we do as a company that excite you? Where do you think that your abilities best lend themselves to being part of the growth of this company?" Those conversations have not been happening, and they need to. There are too many companies out there that—going back to the resume situation—say, "We want people who are entrepreneurial." I love how many job applications say, "We're looking for that entrepreneurial individual." And as soon as you hire them, you put them in a box and say, "That's your job; do your job." Why would you ever hire somebody, ask them to be entrepreneurial, and then put them inside a box? Companies need to have a true understanding: What do they really want? What is their culture? What is their belief in the growth of their people? How do they believe in their people? Are people just a commodity that you're going to use for as long as you have them, spit them out and hire somebody else? There are companies like that. Or there are companies that say, "What's the potential of the individual? How can we inspire this person to grow with us?" Because every employee you lose is costing you a hundred thousand dollars to replace. Better to invest that money to train the person over a lifetime and give them the opportunities to become the person that they're bound to be, and support your organization's growth, inspire other people within your organizations, build your organizations, create more loyal clients—all that comes from having that mentality that people are people. We need to understand what an individual's talents and aspirations are. Some people want to go to a job—there are people who are executive assistants, etc.—that's what they want to do; that's what they want. If that's what they want to do, then you ask them, "How can we make your job better?" But if people have the aspiration to move, change and grow, then give them the ability. Hey, listen, I know some kick-ass executive assistants who, first of all, make a ton of money; and second of all, have all the power, and they are the ear of the CEO. They do phenomenal jobs; I'd never belittle that. That's a position that nobody understands. There is true power and true responsibility being a great EA. But it's also allowing that person to grow into the position and become better at what they do and have more responsibility within the organization.

❝You have to take people's innate skills, their innate abilities, and say, "How can we make this work within our culture?"❞

CC: Nothing lights up an employee more than when you ask them, with genuine curiosity and openness, "Where do you want to go, what do you want to do next, and how can we help you get there?" We put a lot of emphasis on the job of a leader to give clear expectations and to remove barriers to their employees' success. Over time, most leaders have gotten pretty good at the first part, with conveying clear expectations. The more connected they are to the "why" and where they're headed, the easier it is to convey expectations and provide feedback and coaching that keeps them on the right path. The part where most leaders, in my experience, still are woefully deficient is in that second part of removing barriers, which they are in a unique position of power to do. You talk about some of these legacy industries, where people have spent 30, 35 years. I spent about 15 years in the utility industry, and I was still somewhat of a newbie compared to others. We had an annual service awards dinner, where people were getting pins for 40 and 45 years, and there were multiple generations of the same family who grew up at the treatment facility. That's what they knew. And, to your point, some of them stayed in operations, and maybe moved up a little bit and got more complexity in their job, whereas others moved into more of a managerial role. But what was great about spending my close to 15 years there was that I had at least five different career changes. The most profound one was in a direction I never thought I would go, and it was because of the CEO. He was extremely experienced. He was not new to being a CEO; in fact, it was his last CEO assignment before he retired. But he was the best executive I've ever been led by. I was a manager or a director at the time; I was not his direct report. He had come into the company and said his vision was very, very clear: "We are going to be about three things: employees, customers, and efficiency. And if we get those three things right, then the profitability, the innovation, the sustainable growth... all of those other things are going to be fruits from that tree." It was such a simple yet profound message, because everyone could attach some meaning between what they did as their job and at least one of those three pillars of his vision. At the time I was in a communications role, but I was also splitting time over in our customer service department, because they needed some training and some resources. One Friday he sat me down and said, "Claire, I like what I've seen in you, and I see that you've got communications experience and you're also working in customer service. I want you to go home, and think over the weekend about what you want to do next. Then come see me on Monday and let me know." So I thought about it over the weekend, and I came back to him on Monday and said, "I've heard you loud and clear that one of the pillars of your vision is customers. And I would like to commit the next phase of my career to customer service." And he said, "Fantastic. Done." I literally wrote my own job description, because I knew what was important in his vision and where I could contribute what I was good at, what I believed in, what I was passionate about, into a role that I filled for about three years. The takeaway from that is, here's a leader who didn't stand on structure. Yes, you need a certain level of hierarchy. But he deeply believed in putting people in a position where they could contribute their best work, energy and ideas, and to hell with what the job description says, because he didn't pay much attention to that. I know a lot of companies would hear that and say, "Oh no, that would be chaos." How many leaders do you know, with very established hierarchies and long legacies of well-documented job descriptions, who manage by chaos, because they know no other way? So if you're telling me that, if we blow up job descriptions and just put people into positions where they can contribute their best, THAT's going to be chaos, then you're worried about the wrong things.

❝If you're telling me that, if we blow up job descriptions and just put people into positions where they can contribute their best, THAT's going to be chaos, then you're worried about the wrong things.❞

BB: The first thing I hear from that is, this is a phenomenal leader. This is not a manager of people; this is a leader. This is someone who articulates his vision, who's not afraid of losing somebody in order to make sure that person is fulfilling her purpose. There are too many leaders out there who are ill-trained. The Peter Principle still lives and is still rampant throughout the world. We are hired to the level of our incompetence, or we are promoted to the level of our incompetence. It comes down to lack of training. But it also comes down to the fact that we are so afraid of losing power within our own fiefdom that we don't allow people to be the best they can be. We're so afraid of losing our power that we're not going to give a great employee to somebody else, because that might make them better and us worse—instead of saying, "What's the best thing for the organization as a whole? What's the best thing for that individual person? Where is the company going to be best served by this person? Where are their true talents? Are they happy, are they productive, are they engaged?" And if it means moving somebody to a different department or giving them a promotion or retraining them, we're doing whatever needs to be done to make the company better. People need to stop thinking about "my fiefdom versus your fiefdom" or "my budget versus your budget," whether I'm going to get promoted or you're going to get promoted. Guess what? You're going to get promoted if you're the person who's the better leader. If you're the person who inspires people, if you're the one who has the team that absolutely digs in and gets stuff done, and is inspired and motivated, people are going to see that. You're going to say, "Why are these people motivated? Wait a second— the person who's leading them is doing a great job, and he or she is inspiring these people to be their best." Tap, tap, tap on the shoulder comes: "We have a position at the next level. Love to talk to you about it." That's how leaders become better leaders. It's by waking up every single morning and saying, "How can I make my team better? What tools does my team need for them to be better at what they do?" Forget about the ego, forget about "It's all about me," forget about my own self-importance. That stuff has got to go out the window. We need to start thinking about, as you said, How do we take care of employees? How do we take care of customers? If we're taking care of employees and we're taking care of customers, we're living our purpose and we're doing the job that we're supposed to be doing as a company, everybody wins. If you're so worried about your own little fiefdom, if you're so worried about your own little budget, you're thinking too small.

CC: Everything you said resonates loud and clear with me. One of the things you just touched upon is that companies typically promote leaders because they are ambitious versus aspirational. A lot of managers say they "aspire" to leadership. But what they're really saying is, "That's where the money and the power are, and therefore I want that." Versus somebody who instinctively says, "My leadership is defined by the level at which people follow me, and the level to which I am leading them down the right path toward fulfilling our mission." That's an aspirational leader. An ambitious leader sees the leather chair, the compensation, the stock options, and that's why they want to be in that seat. Too often companies promote based on ambition, not on aspiration.

BB: That's having the wrong culture. That's truly a cultural thing. I love watching the dynamic of a C-Suite, because there is only one chair at the top, and that's a CEO position. Watching people who are supposed to be the stewards of the company, the people who are supposed to be there to help guide the long-term vision of the company, stepping on each other's throats to make sure that they are the next CEO. It's the wrong mentality. People below you, the people who look to you as a leader, are watching this every single day and saying, "Why do I want to be part of this if it's just a power game?" If it's all just a power game—yes, money is important; yes, we all want to feel that what we do is being recognized and that people will want to promote us; that's important—but we need to be promoted because that's the right thing. It all comes down to understanding what is the brand story, what is the culture, what is the organization all about? Because if we can do that, we're going to understand the purpose, we're going to understand the vision, everybody's living it, then that's where we need to go forward.

❝It all comes down to understanding what is the brand story, what is the culture, what is the organization all about?❞

QUESTION:

Do the people on your teams have the skills they need to help you get to the next level and beyond? How can you make sure they continue to be productive, engaged contributors over the long term?

_____

_____

_____

_____

_____

_____

_____

_____

_____

QUESTION:

Do the people on your team have the skills they need to help you get to the next level at this end? How can you help them while trying to be efficient in helping them to become better leaders on your staff?

_____

_____

_____

_____

_____

_____

_____

_____

_____

_____

_____

EPISODE 7

THE IMPORTANCE OF YOUR BRAND STORY

CC: We rounded out the last episode with the concept of ambition versus aspiration, watching the social experiment known as the C-Suite, and seeing how the people under the CEO—in companies that are not high functioning—tend to jump all over each other to try to get into that seat next. That's how silos form and get perpetuated. The thought I just wanted to touch upon before we get really deep into the brand story is this: Part of the reason silos are created and exist is because in many companies—and I dare say in most companies—the leaders are still empire builders, which is also a holdover from a previous age that really has no place in modern society. Instead of building empires, they need to be building value. Because that's where true innovation, true competitiveness, and true customer service come from: from the value that you create, put out into the market, and express to prospective clients and employees. It's not "We've got this really big empire and it's growing; won't you be part of that fiefdom?" It's "We've got this amazing story; how would you like to be part of it?" I know that is your passion and your life's work.

❝Part of the reason silos are created and exist is because in many companies... the leaders are still empire builders. Instead of building empires, they need to be building value.❞

BB: I am on a life mission, and life passion, to get rid of mission/vision/values statements. They need to be wiped off the face of the earth. Board retreats need to stop thinking about "We need to create a mission/vision/values statement," and they need to start thinking about a brand story. Let me explain why. The mission/vision/values statements, as they are, are short, pithy statements that get printed on stationery and hung up on the wall as a document somewhere. But they never get lived. They're not remembered. They're not instilled in the people. They're not part of the culture and the DNA of the organization. They're just words. If you take the average employee—even employees that have been with you for 5, 10, 15 years—and you say, "Tell me the mission/vision/values/statement," you'd be hard-pressed to have a dozen people within a large organization that could say them verbatim and tell you what they mean. That's scary, because I'm a big believer of "people plus purpose equals profit." You need to have the purpose, and that is your brand story. Now the brand story takes the mission/vision/values statement and incorporates it into a story format. Because we remember stories. From 10,000 years ago, we still remember stories. Everybody still talks about the flood story. Everybody still talks about the Tower of Babel. People still talk about Adam and Eve. People tell the stories of the pyramids. People tell stories about Native American and Native Canadian culture. There are lots of stories out there. But the reason these stories persist is because they're engaging, they're internalized, people make them their own, and people bring them inside. They understand them, they recall them, and they retell them. Because that happens on a regular basis, they become part of our DNA; they become part of who we are. With that, all of a sudden, the organizations are in a meeting and somebody says, "Well wait a sec; that's not part of our brand story. Why are we doing this? Why are we doing this initiative? Why are we buying this piece of equipment? Why are we going in this direction? Why are we dealing with this customer? It's not part of our brand story. It's not who we are." Heads should snap and people should say, "Oh yeah, wait a second," and everybody knows what they're talking about, because you have a story that says, "This is where we came from. This is our DNA. This is our genesis. This is where the company is. Here are the challenges and opportunities that got us from here to there. Okay? Everybody understands that. Now that we're here, this is who we are, this is what we do, this is why we do it, this is who we do it for and, more importantly, this is why people care." If we can bring that together and then take it onto "This is where we're going, this is how you are part of where we are going, and this is how what you do matters to the company and how you help us succeed," all of a sudden, it doesn't matter what people's roles are in the company; if they can internalize it and they can retell it in their own way, it becomes part of their DNA. They have purpose. They understand from day one and ongoing, because that story needs to be told and retold through meetings and events and town halls. It needs to be lived. When people live it and it's authentic and that story grows, people catch on to it. Then not only do employees get it, but customers and vendors do. Then suddenly the whole DNA of that company elevates. Because then it's not just about price, it's not about the tangible thing, it's about why we do what we do. That's what we need to be focused on as organizations: In the words of Simon Sinek, "It's why we do what we do." Because if we start with why—if we say, "This is who we are, and this is why we do what we do"—everybody can understand that. Because people say, "Oh, okay, there's a purpose behind moving something from point A to point B," instead of just "It's a job for me to move stuff from warehouse A to warehouse B." There's a reason why we keep it in warehouse A and then we bring it in to warehouse B, and this is why we've done it; this is why it's more efficient this way. It gives you a reason to say, "Oh, I get it! Well, what if we did this?" "Oh! We hadn't thought of that." Now we have a reason to move forward. It's an evolving situation. It's fluid. It's something that is built on the people within the company itself. And as there are major changes within the organization, we need to go back and re-communicate that, and we need to re-onboard everybody and be able to say, "Look, our brand story has changed because of COVID-19. We were doing this; now, because these are the challenges we faced, these are the opportunities that we see; we're now going in this direction. "It gives people a sense of purpose. It gives people a sense of direction. It gives people a sense of meaning. So that's the brand story.

"It gives people a sense of purpose. It gives people a sense of direction. It gives people a sense of meaning. That's the brand story."

CC: I have a similar, visceral reaction to a mission statement versus a true mission, which is a purpose, a why—there's such a deep gap between the two. But the more a story is shared, the more it's amplified. I think the difference between a mission statement and a brand story is that a mission statement is not lived. As you say, if anyone in the company can recite it, that's all they're doing; they're not living it. It tends to be finite; it tends to be fixed. A brand story evolves. It should continue to propel and compel you toward your why, but you see yourself folded in the pages of it. You see how you can contribute to it. It is so magnetic for employees and candidates, customers and clients. That concept of being pulled toward a company because of the story it tells and continues to unfold and continues to invite people to be a part of—boy, that's magnetic. I know companies that have spent hundreds of thousands of dollars on outside PR firms that specialize in writing mission statements. It's not that they're not worth the paper they're printed on. But if all they ever do is go on a pretty poster on the wall—"This is our mission, our vision, our values"—and not one person can relate to that or to the overall purpose, it's a waste of money. Last episode, I shared the story of this amazing CEO I had the good fortune to work with, who sat me down and said, "Forget what job description you have now; forget what job description you might be assigned later. What do you want to do? How can you best contribute to the company?" It was easy for me to find my place, because he had been so clear about what the company was going to be about. He retired as CEO about 12, maybe 15 years ago, and, as I said, this was in a utility industry, where you have a lot of long-term employees. To this day, if you walked up to any of those employees who were there at the time that he was CEO, and you asked them what his three key priorities were, I guarantee you at least 98% of them would be able to tell you they were employees, customers and efficiency. That's the lasting legacy. That's not the mission statement or the statement of values. But those were the guiding principles upon which every single person, from the frontline union employee to the C-Suite, could attach meaning.

❝The more a story is shared, the more it's amplified.❞

BB: They were living it. Not only was he saying that these things are important; he was living it. How he treated his employees was done this way. How he treated their customers was this way. How he set the priorities of the company were based on those three tenets. Because the company is living those three words, it becomes ingrained into everybody's mind. They believe it's not just words on a page; it's an actual, living philosophy. I have a customer from years ago—they're a multi-multi-million-dollar organization across Canada now—that sells heavy farm equipment. The genesis of the story is four generations of a family living on the same farm in rural Saskatchewan. It's understanding the trials, tribulations and challenges they had on that rural farm—growing up through the Depression and everything that went on—that gave him the impetus to start this company. It's that story that he tells every single employee—and they are an enormous company now—but he's the one who continues to tell that story when a new employee is onboarded. It's his passion to tell every new employee about his own humble roots on this rural farm in Saskatchewan, and the challenges that led him to create this company that has become enormously successful. But everybody can tell that story. I can walk into any branch anywhere in Canada and ask any employee what the genesis of the company is, what the brand story is, and every single person could tell it. Because they all believe it, and they live it. The values of the company, how they make decisions, and who their customers are and are not, are all based on that brand story. His attitude is, "We are not going to deal with people who are unethical, and we are not going to deal with people who are untrustworthy. It doesn't matter how much money you have; I don't care how big you are. If you don't fit into our ethical standards as a company, we're not doing business with you." He's proven that a few times over. When you say it, it's one thing; when you do it, it's completely different. And when all of a sudden, employees see you living your brand as an organization, they go, "Okay, they mean it. I can rally behind this. This is not just words on a page; these are people stepping up and actually living their brand story." That's when a company goes from good to great.

CC: When you see a company, such as that one, that is truly, genuinely living its brand, that brand story came out from within; they didn't pay someone to observe them and then put some pretty words around what they saw.

What's interesting about that pivot you just described was, because this company is so in touch with who they are, and very clear on how to express that, they don't stand up and say, "This is what we do." They say, "This is what we won't tolerate in anyone who wants to come work with us or for us." That's a really significant pivot. When you can get to a brand story that is that genuine and that magnetic, it becomes a screening process for clients to even approach you, versus the opposite. When we first were talking about brand story—and I think we have talked about that since our very first conversation in this series—one of the things that we talked about was that everybody around the globe right now has a golden opportunity to incorporate this shared experience, that we have through COVID-19, into their brand story. I know you've got some very passionate opinions about how companies should do that, and why they should not shy away from incorporating this globally shared experience into their brand story.

BB: For me, the struggle is part of your brand story. If your brand story is "We started our company in 2003, and in 2020 we're worth a hundred million dollars," nobody cares. The end.

CC: "We kept the lights on. Yay."

BB: Yeah. Our brand story is built not only on the good, but on the bad and the ugly, and what we learned from the bad and the ugly. Take a look at it as the Lion King. If we're going to go into the classic brand story, it's the hero's journey. People want to know the journey of the hero. They want to rally behind the hero, but they know the hero is not perfect. It's the first time you look at your parents and you go, "They're not as perfect as I thought they were. Okay, I still love them." It's being able to understand that the company that you work for, and the company that you work with, and the companies that you buy from are not perfect. They're going to make mistakes, they're going to have challenges, they're going to have frustrations, they're going to have missteps, and they're going to go off in directions. Like a new Coke—look at what happened with new Coke. But we all come back. Because people at Coke said, "We're sorry. We made a mistake. We went in a different direction that was away from our brand purpose, that was away from who we are. We thank you for the trust that you've given us over the years. We're re-evaluating, and then this is how we're going to move forward." I think there's something extremely powerful in that, both internally and externally in a company, to understand that there is fallibility. That fallibility makes us better. Being able to make mistakes and say, "That didn't work out. Okay, what did we learn from it? Let's not point fingers; let's not lay blame. It's not Joe's fault, it's not Mary's fault, it's not Alan's fault. As an organization, we made this decision that we were going to move forward. What happened? What did we learn from it? What came out of it that was good? What came out of it that was bad? How do we fix this? How do we move forward?" The more we can articulate that, the more we can articulate the challenges that we went through, the more people around us are going to rally around us. Because people root for the underdog. People want to see people who have gone through the trials or tribulations. That's why I hate all these internet people who say, "I can make you a millionaire," and all you see is the Ferrari and the jet. You look at them and think, "Why should I follow you? If all I see is the success, without the failure that went along with it, how do I know that you've actually been down that same deep, dark hole that I've been down? How do I know that you know how to get out of that hole? Or did you read a few things on the internet and then create a brand that says," I know everything?" Have you actually been down that hole? Have you actually sat there and had the water rain down on your head, trying to figure out how to scrape your way out of that hole? If you haven't, how can you instill confidence in your clients and how to help them out of that hole? That's how we believe in each other. That's how we grow.

❝There's something extremely powerful in that, both internally and externally in a company, to understand that there is fallibility. And that fallibility makes us better.❞

CC: It reminds me of the old movie sets, the Wild West scenes, where you had the town, and the saloon, and the general store. But it was actually a facade: the storefronts were just held up by two-by-fours. I think of those companies that put forth a brand statement that is really just a facade of their success, versus ones who have deeply embedded value systems—not flowery value statements. You attract what you emanate. So if all I am is a facade of success, then really, ultimately, if I'm looking for new employees, the only ones I'm going to be able to attract, let alone retain, are those who can put up a good facade. That's where cultures of blaming, of ignoring mistakes, and of leaders who do not admit to their vulnerability arise. They're not three-dimensional. Therefore, they are not going to be successful in the long run—at least not in the ways that you and I define success. On the flip side of that, a genuine, deeply felt, purely embedded brand story begets brand loyalty. That's something you can't buy. You can only pull people into your orbit because you are, as you said, living your values, living your brand, and allowing those people who get it—those people who subscribe to that same system of value and in the hardscrabble "It's as much about our successes as learning from our failures"—you attract them and give them every opportunity to contribute chapters and character depth to the story.

❝A genuine, deeply felt, purely embedded brand story begets brand loyalty.❞

QUESTION:

What is the story that you tell within your organization? How do others within your organization tell the same story? Are those stories consistent? Why or why not?

_____

_____

_____

_____

_____

_____

_____

_____

_____

EPISODE 8

ARE YOU TRULY DISRUPTIVE?

CC: You and I have very similar philosophies, although different perspectives, on this whole business of ours that we do. In an earlier episode, I ranted about silos, and how companies perpetuate that. But you and I, offline, had talked about this concept of "disruptive" and "market disruption." Before COVID-19 impacted our lives, everybody was inundated with these consultants, coaches, gurus and masterminds around "disrupting your market" and "disrupting your career" and blah blah blah. It ticked me off a lot. Then when you and I were talking about it, I thought I was mad about the phrase; but you really got into a rant—which I loved, by the way. So we'll just go back into that moment, because, to me, it's very irresponsible for someone to come in and try to incite disruption and not have the wherewithal or the social responsibility to guide that in a constructive way. That's the reason that we're where we are in terms of this disruptive climate. So I'm going to tee you up and watch you go.

BB: So up on the soapbox I go. To me, the word "disruption" has been so overused. It's so misused that it just drives me crazy. It's gotten down to disruptive underwear, disruptive coffee mugs, disruptive bandannas.

CC: Oh yeah. You must have disruptive underwear.

BB: Right? What does that even mean? People are using the word "disruptive" to mean basically anything. Anytime something shifts a little bit to the left, a little bit to the right, and it's new and exciting, it's disruptive. The problem is... it's NOT disruptive. COVID-19 is disruptive. 9/11 was disruptive. The war in Syria is disruptive. The war in Afghanistan is disruptive. World famines are disruptive. There are things that change the fabric of society, they change the fabric of our lives, they mark a moment in time where we say, "We can't go back; we need to find a way forward." That, to me, is disruptive. The people who are using "disruptive" as a marketing term to say "We're new and innovative" need to find another word. Because everybody has overused and misused the word "disruptive" to the point where it doesn't mean anything anymore. I go down to Vegas every year for a promotional marketing show, and picture this: The Mandalay Bay convention center is one floor, with a million square feet, 13 and a half miles of show floor, 750,000 different promotional products, and everybody screaming that their stuff is new and disruptive. I met somebody who told me that because their coffee mug kept their coffee warm 10-20 minutes longer, that was disruptive. I had people telling me that because they've come up with a new, innovative color, that was disruptive. Because they came up with a different type of lanyard, it was disruptive. There are things that are earth-shatteringly important enough that they're going to change our lives, that they're going to change the way that we think about things and the way that we react to things. That's what being truly and absolutely disruptive is all about. When Microsoft created Windows, when the Apple computer came along and changed the fabric of society, when DOS 3.3 came along and all of a sudden when you were coding, you could actually look forward and backward instead of having to write code and say "Oh, I made a mistake," and had to go all the way to the end, save, go back into the code, go find the line again, and then be able to change the code, save it, and then go forward again—when you could go forward and backward, that was innovative; that was exciting. That might have been disruptive in the day, it changed the way people actually did their lives, made their lives better, enabled people to be far more effective and more efficient, and allowed them to be more innovative as they moved forward, because they were able to move in a different way and think in a different way. That's disruptive. So we need to think as companies, "Are we being disruptive? Are we truly changing the fabric of the world? Or are we just using this word trying to get somebody's attention? Are we adding noise to the universe, or are we adding value?" There are too many people who are making noise out there and saying that they're creating value. We need to create total value. That's where we need to be as organizations. So off I come off my soapbox, and I leave it to you to take it from here.

❝We need to think as companies, "Are we adding noise to the universe, or are we adding value?"❞

CC: Ben, I haven't seen you that worked up since we tackled the topic of the mission statement. And it's for the exact same reasons: People use and misuse those words, that phrase, to the detriment of everyone, because they just give a bad name to those who truly are changing the world. So yeah, this concept of disruption, the examples that you used of truly disruptive entrants into the market…. When I'm on my deathbed, if my legacy is that I put out into the market a brand new lanyard, I want you to find me and I want you to politely or emphatically correct me. Because that's not going to be my legacy, a disruptive new lanyard.

BB: But it could be new, and it could be innovative.

CC: Oh yeah. If it's a hologram and it changes colors.

BB: It could have LED lights or something that blinks on and off. That's kind of cool. But that's all it is.

CC: Exactly. But, to your point, it comes back to how we're defining things. These "disruptors"—who really aren't— are like those old Wild West Hollywood sets we were talking about, where the facade of the saloon and the general store were propped up with two-by-fours behind the scenes. These disruptors are all flash—excuse me, the ones who use that term "disruptor," not the genuine disruptors. The Steve Jobs and Elon Musks of the world— and yes, I'm setting a very high bar for those who would call themselves disruptors—you'd better be on that level. Otherwise you're just an interrupter. You're going to be shushed and escorted from the room. So there's true disruption—as you said, COVID-19 being one. I'm on the East Coast; Superstorm Sandy was a huge one. 9/11, obviously. Huge disruptors that we did not necessarily see coming; it was not in the plans or in the strategy for any of us who were impacted. But just like COVID-19, it forced us to reevaluate, to reassess, what we have believed is truly important—yes, on a personal level, but as a business. What were things we were chasing that we had convinced ourselves were business-relevant? What were processes we were continuing to follow that we had convinced ourselves were business-critical that now, because of this latest disruption, we were forced to do without—and yet we're still functioning, we're still getting everything done? So that, to me, is a disruption that can cause feelings of lack of control, but again are all these opportunities for companies and business leaders to say, "We thought we had planned for something like this, but we really didn't, we were caught a bit unaware. How do we learn from it, how do we get better as a result of it, and how do we make sure we are continuing to move forward toward our why?"

BB: It's interesting that you say that, because you say that a true disruption is something that we never saw coming and changed our life because of it. It's like the new batteries that are coming out today that all of a sudden go from being able to power something for 10 minutes to being able to power something for 10 hours, and the millions and millions of lives that are changed because of that innovation. It is truly amazing. Look at the Elon Musks, the Bill Gates, the Steve Jobs of the world. Even take a look at Mark Zuckerberg. Zuckerberg's vision of Facebook changed the fabric of the world, in how we communicate, engage and interact, and what media truly is. What is media today? How do we communicate it, add value and form our opinions? It's taken this hierarchical media empire and flattened it so everybody has a microphone. It's truly disruptive. Those are the truly disruptive things in the world. But we need to say, as an organization, are we truly at that level? And it's okay if we're not. There are millions and millions of businesses around the world that are not disruptive, that add value, that help millions, if not billions, of clients, that take care of people, that are worth our trust and allow us to make our lives better. But they're truly not disruptive in what they do. As businesses and as leaders, we need to say, "What is our pocket? What do we truly do? Who are the people we truly serve?" It's not everybody with a Visa card. It is absolutely not everybody with a pulse; that is not our customer base. The question is, "Who are the people that we truly add value to, and why do we add value to them? Why do these people care, and how do we communicate with them in a way that resonates with them?" It has to stop being about us, and it has to start being about our people—whether it's our internal people or our external people—and we need to say, "How are we adding value as a company?" Where you came from in the very beginning of this: It's all about adding value. It doesn't have to be disruptive. It doesn't have to be always innovative. Sometimes, if you're in a rush and somebody gets your coffee effectively and efficiently and with a smile, that can make your entire day. When you were in a rush, and you were panicked, and somebody smiled, said a couple of quick words to you, and got you in and out, and you were able to move on with your day efficiently so you didn't have the hangries anymore—that's a great business. It's not innovative, it's not disruptive, but it's full of people who care. I'll take people who care any day of the week over something that is touting itself as disruptive and, as you said, is truly interruptive at best.

❝There are millions and millions of businesses around the world that are not disruptive, that add value, that help millions, if not billions, of clients, that take care of people, that are worth our trust and allow us to make our lives better.❞

CC: What a great challenge for leaders. Because, as you said, as a business leader, not every idea or initiative is innovative and world-changing. Not everyone is Elon Musk. People thought he was nuts—which is usually a sign that you're onto something—when he said, "We're going to put people on Mars." It wasn't enough that he co-founded PayPal. It wasn't enough that he went out and said, "I'm going to make electric cars." And it wasn't enough for him to make commercial rockets that can be reused. Now he says that these were all steps, but we're going to get to Mars and colonize it. As kids, we watched the old sci-fi movies, and now it might happen in our lifetimes. Might. But I said before, I set the bar high: We're talking about Steve Jobs, and Elon Musk, and Bill Gates. Not every leader has to change the world at that level. But your role does shape the world of the people who work for you. As you said, you can disrupt, you can shape, you can impact that world for the better—or you can do the opposite. I had an argument once with my direct boss—and it didn't go well, so I stopped arguing with him—but he had said something in a meeting that really shook up his team. I went to him afterwards and said, "The morale with the team took a hit there." He said, "Well, that's not the way I meant for my message to come out." I said, "But it did." He said, "I'm not responsible for how my message is received." So I responded, "You are a leader. You absolutely have a responsibility for how your message is received." Some leaders don't care. They say, "I've gotten to where I am, I'm in power, I have control, I have the leather chair, and you can take my message the way you want to take it." A true leader makes sure that the message is heard, understood, received the right way, and acted upon in the direction that moves us toward our why. It's honestly as simple as that.

❝A true leader makes sure that the message is heard, understood, received the right way, and acted upon in the direction that moves us toward our why. It's honestly as simple as that.❞

BB: It's true. How many companies, when I ask, "Well, do your people understand your mission/vision/values," say, "Well, they should: We talk about it once a year at our corporate retreat." But leaders have two choices: They can take the rocks, and they can hold them close to their chests; or they can drop them in the water and create the ripples. The true leaders are the ones who are dropping the pebbles, letting them fall where they lie, and watching the ripples occur. I will never change the world. I never will. I'm never going to be President; I'm never going to be Elon Musk; I'm never going to be Bill Gates. But I can change MY corner of the world. I can influence those whom I can influence. I mentor at the universities. Every semester it's me in front of 200 kids, and I get to instill my vision on what leadership, what true leadership, is. By doing that, hopefully 5 or 10 or even 30 of them will take that and internalize it, and it will make them better people. If they take that and then become better leaders themselves, an amazing ripple effect happens. All I can do is control my corner of the world. My buddy Peter Turin says, "It's easy to do, and it's easy not to do." I love that philosophy of "easy to do, easy not to do." Because you can either hold the rock next to your chest and say, "This is my knowledge, I'm going to keep it, nobody can have it," or you can say, "How can I help other people be better?" I choose, and I hope that the leaders listening to this choose, to empower their team and help their team be better. Because when they do that, they're going to inspire greatness in others that they probably never even realize what will happen next.

CC: During our last episode, you used the phrase "good to great," and of course you're familiar with the book by Jim Collins. Collins talks at great length about how many leaders think the true mark of their success is that things fall apart without them. But the direct opposite is true: The truly great companies are the ones that not only continue to survive and keep the lights on after the Jack Welch or the Bill Gates has left, but continue to thrive, evolve, improve, move toward that why, and shape a brand story that is positive and gives back. Your metaphor of the rocks rings so true for me, because I do think a lot of leaders hold on to that insecurity that individual contributors do, which is, "If I share my knowledge, I become less valuable. If other people know what I know, then I become expendable." Well, I have news for you: Whether you're a frontline worker or the CEO, everyone at some point is replaceable. So rather than worry about being replaced because you are stingy with your knowledge, look at it as: You were never meant to hide what you're truly talented at, what you deeply know, what you can genuinely give, from the world, or your corner of it. It is your obligation, especially as a leader, to share what you know, what you have, what you can do. Again, it goes back to what we talked about last time: Are you pursuing a leadership track because you're ambitious or because you're aspirational? If you're ambitious, you tend to hold on to knowledge as your competitive edge; if you're aspirational, you see it as a gift to share with the world.

❝If you're ambitious, you tend to hold on to knowledge as your competitive edge; if you're aspirational, you see it as a gift to share with the world.❞

BB: I love that. I'm just going to say one more thing to bring this full circle. Very few leaders are disruptive; very few leaders are going to change the world in ways that other people haven't thought about. But millions, if not billions, of leaders out there are going to make people's lives better, and are going to help make things better, and change little things about how people live their lives. That should never be belittled. If you can change one person's life, or you can make one person's life better, if you can help one person achieve greatness, you've been an amazing leader. That's what we need to be thinking of. We don't have to always hit the home run; we need to get on base. We basically need to connect with people. We need to make sure that people go around the bases and score. We may not be the one who hits the home run or drives in the winning run; but when we're there, when it happens, we get to be part of it. That's what leaders need to be thinking.

QUESTION:

Are you truly disruptive? Are you an innovator, or are you simply a company with a good product and a great customer experience with loyal clients? How are you evaluating who you truly are and the value you bring to others?

_____

_____

_____

_____

_____

_____

_____

_____

_____

EPISODE 9

THE CUSTOMER EXPERIENCE

CC: Ben, I really should be concerned, as your friend, when you go on a rant. But it's too entertaining for me. So I thought I would stoke the embers and get you on another one.

BB: Absolutely.

CC: Cool. So, a couple episodes ago, we did a deep dive into the brand story. Part of what you talked about was the fact that, at its core, it's the hero's journey; and that the reason we like heroes, and are attracted to heroes, is not because they are perfect, but because they are flawed, that they make mistakes. And when we translated that into business, we said all companies make mistakes, and they are in essence human, because they are run, staffed and built by humans. You recently shared with me a very unsatisfactory experience that you had as a customer. So I thought we could dive into the customer experience, starting from that story and the experience that you had.

BB: It's not the fact that people fail that we get excited about; we get excited that people fail and then recover. It's that recovery that makes the true hero. It's like, "I did something wrong. Something blew up; something didn't go right. I dusted myself off, looked around, figured out

what went wrong, reevaluated, and moved forward."
That's what's really key. I tell customers all the time, "I'm
not perfect. I'm going to make a mistake. I'm going to
do something that's going to frustrate you, I'm going
to do something that is going to be something that you
didn't exactly want to have happen." It's going to happen
sometime in the 10-, 15-, 20-year relationship. A lot of my
relationships are that long. I'm human. Tell me. Give me
the opportunity to understand how I've made something
wrong and allow me to fix it. That's the key thing. If we
can fix things, if we can say, "Mea culpa. I'm sorry. I'm
really sorry. I didn't mean to do this, or this happened,
and here's how we can fix this that's going to be good
for you." That's all we can ever expect of people. If we
expect everybody to be perfect 100% of the time, we're
going to bounce from vendor to vendor for the rest of our
lives. However, If we can build relationships, and know
that 95-99% of the time, these guys and girls are great,
but every once in a while they're going to mess up and
something's going to happen, but you know if something
does happen, they're going to fix it, that's a relationship.
We need to be thinking about that, both outside and
inside of the company, as I mention this story. Now,
this story goes back probably 5 or 6 months. It probably
started sometime in late 2019. I was working for one of
my customers, and we were putting a project together.
This project had 7 or 8 components that had to come
from 7 or 8 different suppliers. So we were amalgamating
a whole bunch of stuff. It had to be there at a certain time
on a certain date, because it was for government year-
end, and if it's not delivered by a certain time and it's not
invoiced properly, the government goes crazy and they

can't put it on this year's budget, so they lose their budget for next year. So there are all these things to consider. Now, this particular part of the program was coming from the United States. I am maniacal about what I put on my purchase order—especially when it comes from the US, and this was something that was made in the US. You need to put a NAFTA with this, you need to have the right paperwork with it, the right documentation, the invoice with it, so it gets through the border more easily. Well, not only did they not read my paperwork, but they didn't charge my brokerage account, they shipped it to the wrong address, they didn't put the NAFTA in there—there were a hundred things that they did wrong. If they had just called me, or at least followed the instructions on the purchase order, it would have been fine. But we fixed it: We got it to the customer on time, the customer never knew, the customer's account never got charged—we reversed it before they had a chance to get the invoice—so the customer was no worse because of this. But it took an enormous amount of my time to fix the mistake. We came to a resolution: They were going to pay for the shipping. Great. Now, the problem was, for the next three months, on the 15th of every month, I got another invoice for that shipping amount, saying, "You owe this, and it's now 30 days overdue, now 60 days overdue, now 90 days overdue." Every time I got this, I called up the manager on shift and I said, "Hey, listen, I got another invoice." "Oh, no, we're going to take care of it, don't worry about it, it's fine, we're going to take care of it." But it never got taken care of. Well, they finally said, "No, no, we're going to get you a credit memo."

Just the other day, another invoice showed up. I didn't even open it. I sent it back, and I went online and found out who the owner of the company was, and I CC'd them on my email voicing my displeasure at how this whole process was going along. Well, turns out, two things: One, it actually WAS a credit memo, but it said "invoice" on it; it's a "reversed invoice." If it had just said "credit memo" in the subject line of the email, I would have been fine, and we would have solved this whole thing in about 2.3 seconds. Fine. I finally got my credit memo for this thing. It's over; it's done. Nothing happened for about 24-48 hours. Then, did I get a phone call from the owner of the company? NO! And my displeasure in this email was quite extensive; there was no ambiguity in the displeasure that I was facing after 90 days of dealing with this stuff. But instead I got a phone call, not even the customer service manager, but from the inside sales manager. The first thing I said to her was, "Look, I'm going on this Zoom call in about four minutes." And she started talking. Not, "Can I call you back?" Not, "Is there a better time?" She just kept talking. It was as if she was doing me a favor by calling me; that she didn't have to call me; that she was going above and beyond. She made me feel like she was going above and beyond, calling me to let me know that, "Well, this is the first time we've ever had a problem with somebody, with the credit memo being called an invoice." So it's obviously my fault.

❝It's not the fact that people fail that we get excited about; we get excited that people fail and then recover. It's that recovery that makes the true hero. ❞

CC: Sure. I hope you got her mailing address so you can send her the gold star that she so clearly deserves.

BB: I'm seriously thinking about buying a few books on customer experience and mailing them to her. Collect. I'm thinking about putting it on an invoice, parcel-paid directly to her. Actually, that's not a bad idea; we may actually do that.

CC: At least charge her for the shipping.

BB: Exactly. I don't mind paying for the books, but charge her for the shipping.

CC: We call that a proportional response.

BB: Exactly. There are so many holes in this story from a leadership point of view. Their whole comment was, "Well, because of COVID-19 this" and "COVID-19 that." Get over it. Customers are customers are customers. Customers are willing to work with you if you communicate properly. If you make a mistake and you fix it, if you let people know what the challenges are and how you're working to solve it, and you solve it, then that's fine; we can work with you on that. But when you ghost us, when you make it feel like it's our fault, when you blame a worldwide situation without having any resolution for this, you really need to give your head a shake. Because leadership needs to look at this and say, "Alright, do we have the right people in place, and are our people trained properly to deal with customer experience?" Because this issue showed serious holes. There is an absence in leadership by the owner of the company not actually picking up the phone himself and calling me. If I had gotten that email, I would have been on a phone call. I would have gone downstairs, gotten the information, found out what exactly happened, and been on a phone call in about half an hour. But that's not what happened. I got a phone call—not from the vice president of sales, not from the vice president of marketing, not from the owner of the company, not even from a customer service manager—but from the inside sales manager, who made me feel that this was my fault. We, as companies, need to start thinking about this. Because customer experience is going to be a gold standard moving forward. That's how we're going to be able to differentiate ourselves as companies. If we're not doing that, if we're not developing a customer experience model that is designed first, last and only with the customer in mind, and "How do we wow this customer time after time after time?" and "How do we enable our people and develop leaders that believe that customer service and customer experience is number one?" we're in serious trouble as companies. As leaders, now is the time we need to start looking at what policies, what procedures, what opportunities, what people do we have in place, what training have we done to make sure that our teams are full of the right people doing the right things at the right time, and empowered to do so to be able to make sure our customers are taken care of? Because if we don't, we become another low-cost, low-value commodity that literally is easily replaced and easily forgotten. So I want to step off my soapbox. But it all comes down to leadership and communication. It all comes down to setting a vision and living that vision within the company.

❝Customer experience is going to be a gold standard moving forward. That's how we're going to be able to differentiate ourselves as companies.❞

CC: You are 100% right. The employees—especially those who are on the front lines, who interact with the customers—are only as good as the leadership at the top. So if you have one bad apple—the saying of "One bad apple spoils the bunch—well, how did it get to that place? We talked about how every human makes mistakes. I remember, very distinctly, my fourth-grade teacher saying, "There is a reason there are erasers on pencils: because everyone makes mistakes."

❝The employees—especially those who are on the front lines, who interact with the customers—are only as good as the leadership at the top.❞

BB: I want one on my golf pencil.

CC: Why don't they put one on the golf pencil?? Now you're going to get me on a soapbox; I totally agree with you. But that always stuck with me because I thought, "You're right. You're allowed to make a mistake; everyone makes them." The differentiator—especially in business and especially in leadership—is the recovery. How do we make up for that mistake? You talk about the need for training: Where is the breakdown? When there's a breakdown in the "how"—the processes we follow, the scripts we follow as a customer service rep—those breakdowns in the how are exacerbated when there's a disconnect with the "why." The why has to be fueled, it has to be fed, and it has to be reinforced from the top down. I often think about the company Zappos. Tony Hsieh, the CEO of Zappos, has a very clear picture in his mind of what Zappos will always be about. It's one of the most, if not <u>the</u> most, customer-centric companies I've ever interacted with. I've interacted as a consumer, and I've met Tony Hsieh in person. Every person who joins Zappos as an employee spends the first two weeks in a customer service center in Arkansas. They learn from the back office, they interact with customers, they understand the impact of what they do—which isn't just that they sell shoes and offer free shipping each way— they bring happiness to their customers. You just brought up a word that has been key for us in past conversations: "empower." When a mistake is made, their customer service reps are empowered to make it right. They have a lot of latitude and leeway, and autonomy and authority, to refund a customer, to send a different type of a shoe, to help a customer, to fix what breaks down. Because even in a company as customer- and culture-centric as Zappos, they know that something is going to break down at some point.

❝Those breakdowns in the "how" are exacerbated when there's a disconnect with the "why." And the why has to be fueled, it has to be fed, and it has to be reinforced from the top down.❞

BB: And it will. When you're selling tens of thousands of shoes a month—if not hundreds of thousands of shoes a month—something is going to go wrong. The wrong color's going to get shipped, the wrong size is going to get shipped…. There are a million things that can happen.

CC: I remember a story he told—several years ago—about a man who called Zappos. He was very upset because his wife had ordered a pair of shoes, but she had unexpectedly passed away. The shoes arrived shortly after her death. He was so emotional about it, and he said, "I don't know what to do with these shoes." Well, the customer service rep didn't say, "Can you hold, please, while I go get somebody better qualified to resolve this?" This is the frontline customer service rep, who said, "I want you to just return the shoes and we're going to refund you." THEN he sent flowers to the man on behalf of Zappos. He didn't have to get approval; he knew that was the right thing to do. Why was that the right thing to do? Not just because it was in his nature to do the right thing, but because he was brought on, trained, communicated with, respected and empowered enough to do the right thing, and to feel that he had the power to fix things. I think a lot of companies make that misstep, by withholding that empowerment. They say, "You're the front line; you're going to take all the angry phone calls." I've worked in a call center; I know that these guys are taking bullets all the time, and they go home with shrapnel from some of these customers. If you don't empower them to resolve at least a certain level of grievance, what you end up saying to that customer service rep is, "All you're good for is taking the hits; but I'm going to come in and be the white knight. I'm going to be the one who resolves it to the customer's satisfaction." You take that power away from them. It's no wonder that customer service is one of the hardest jobs in any business, if the company doesn't connect their why with their how.

BB: There are three different things that I want to emphasize here. The first is the fact that every single employee starts off at the frontline. I don't care if you're the CFO, I don't care if you're the janitor—everybody within the company sits in a customer experience chair and fields those phone calls. So they have a great idea: Whether you're going to be in operations, shipping, marketing or sales, you sit there for two weeks, and you listen to real customers every single day. Quite honestly, I think that the C-Suite and senior management should do this once a month, or at least once a quarter. Everybody within any organization—if you have a customer service line and you have people that actually sit there and listen to customer service complaints every single day—every single senior person within your company should take time, even if it's four hours a month, to talk to customers. That would be so empowering to be able to understand where the frustrations really lie. It really comes down to leadership empowering people to be able to do the things they need to do. I love the fact that the guy sent flowers. If I interact with a customer experience person who's done a great job, I'm a big believer of saying, "Do me a favor: Can you patch your boss onto the call?" "Why?" "Because I want to tell them what a great job you did." I don't want to fill out your survey—I WILL fill out your survey, and I absolutely do—but I want to say, "Thank you," and I want to say it in a way that's not only meaningful to them, but that their boss understands what a great job they're doing. Because, unfortunately, you're right: These customer experience and customer service people get yelled at day after day, hour after hour, week after week, year after year, and all they hear, 99 times out of a hundred, is, "Why can't you do this?" or "Why won't this happen?" Then all of a sudden they're disempowered or hear, "I want to speak to your manager." Then—you're right— that manager comes in and is that white knight who fixes the problem. But you feel like, "I could have done that just as easily, but I don't have the power to do that." That disengages your staff. I don't know how many times, when I know I'm going to get into a fight with people, I'll say, "Send me to your customer experience team, because I know it's a team that's designed for that dispute resolution, and they actually have the empowerment to do it." Especially with telcos: The frontline people, the customer service people, can make one decision; and the customer experience people, when they're afraid you're going to leave, they can make another decision. So why am I bothering to deal with the frontline people if I know they're not empowered to make a decision, to be able to do the things I need them to do? If they WERE empowered, if I could have a conversation with them and know they had the training, leadership, empowerment and trust of management to be able to make reasonable decisions that were in the best interest of the customer and the company, then I would deal with them. But when you know that's not reality—when the companies are not training, empowering, trusting or leading their people properly—that's when companies break down. That's why you'll just say, "Well, it doesn't matter; we'll go from telco X to telco Y to telco Z." It doesn't really matter because they're all about the same price; they all offer about the same service. So I leave this phone company and go somewhere else. Big deal. Who cares? In two years, guess what? Since I can port my number back, maybe I'll go back to the one that I was with two years ago, because these guys have ticked me off now. We've commoditized the company by not empowering our people, by not training them, by not trusting them. And that comes down to a lack of leadership and communication.

❝We've commoditized the company by not empowering our people, by not training them, by not trusting them. And that comes down to a lack of leadership and communication.❞

CC: The experience of buying a car is very telling in this respect. Unless you are buying a very highly specialized vehicle, a Ford is a Ford; a Honda is a Honda. If I have three dealerships within a 25-mile radius from which to buy the car—that I've already researched and figured out that I want—what's going to make the decision for me? It's not necessarily the closest one; it's the one that has the best ratings—not from their sales team, but from their service department. The sale takes one day. It's a long day—I just bought a car a couple months ago, I knew the car that I wanted, I test drove it, I loved it, and I still couldn't get out of there in less than 6 hours. But I went to that particular dealership because it had a good reputation for service. You brought up a good point earlier: Seldom do customers reach out and contact customer experience when they've had a good interaction. Well, how can we change that? We can change it, as you say, by empowering those people on the front lines. But the rotational aspect is also key in changing the tide. If more companies insisted and required that every single person, from the C-Suite on down, spent their first two weeks in customer service, fielding calls or the very least listening in on calls, and seeing how they are—what's the trend, what are customers complaining about, what are they interested in, what is the resolution—one of the things that happens is, that one percent or five percent of the time that it's a positive customer call, they're going to start to see the impact that they make. What they're also going to do is, when they rotate out of there and go to their "normal role" or back to the C-Suite or wherever, they really have a much clearer, tangible idea of how the decisions they make, the actions they take, the things that they do, and the things that they don't do impact the customer at the end. The customer service representatives are often the only impression that a customer has of your company and your brand. Unless those customers have the opportunity to meet with the CEO—and that person can be as charismatic as they want—but if the why is not connected to the how and embedded in the who, then it doesn't matter how charismatic your CEO is. He's that Wild West facade that we keep talking about: He's propped up by two-by-fours. Because it's the people on the front lines who carry your message and build your brand. The other thing that your story of this inside sales manager—who must have drawn the short straw to call you—reminds me of is this: As leaders, frontline employees, customer service reps, etc., we have an obligation to own our flaws. I have had a past life as a customer relations director, so I didn't get to talk to the customers until they were really whipped up into a frenzy. But there's this opportunity you get when you can turn them around, and you can go back to the customer service rep and thank them for their hard work and doing what they do. But the impact of the customer experience, just getting somebody to say, "We screwed up, we take ownership of that, and we're sorry for it." There are going to be times when we make mistakes as companies, as leaders, that we can't fix, that we can't turn around, that won't make up for the damage. But sometimes all a customer wants to hear is, "We're really sorry."

❝As leaders, frontline employees, customer service reps, etc., we have an obligation to own our flaws.❞

BB: And mean it. And MEAN it.

CC: And mean it! Make sure you're genuine and authentic. I've had interactions as a customer—usually with an airline, where I've gotten bumped or something else happened—where all I want them to say, after they tell me, "We can't do anything about it," is, "I'm sorry." I just need to hear those two words. But you can see in their face that they're dug in, and they won't. That is such a huge disconnect for that company's brand.

BB: I want to take this to a different level. Yes, we have to take care of our customers. Having every employee sitting on a customer service call, and understanding things from the customer's point of view, is enormous. But let's take this internally. What if every employee had to spend a week, or a day, job shadowing people in the different departments? What if marketing had to go out with sales, and sales had to spend time in ops or finance or on the production floor and actually do the job? Can you imagine if salespeople actually understood the process from start to finish of what it actually took to make a part? Not only would they not promise the impossible—because there's a commission at the end of it—but they'd also be far more intelligent talking to customers about the process. Marketing would understand sales better, sales would understand marketing better, everybody would understand finance, finance would understand what other people do. If we can set up a system of cross-training, not only does that make our people more valuable—God forbid if there's a tragedy, something happens and somebody else has to step in—because you're cross-trained, but it gives you a far better understanding of the motivations of the other departments. And it gets rid of silos. It gets rid of the "us versus them." It allows people to function as one, solid team that's focused on the customer, because we understand what it takes for other people within the company to do their job, to serve the customer. Because we're all looking at the customer differently.

CC: This is where siloed leadership has gotten us. You relayed a story previously, about going to a conference years ago, where they had sales in one part of the conference room and ops in the other, and they had very different messages, very different whys, very different purposes that they were incentivized around. It's the reason that I do so much work with senior leadership and executive leadership and the C-Suite to bring them together out of their silos, and really open their eyes to: What you do in your silo impacts the ability, the brand, the capability, and the ultimate outcome of THEIR silo. If only you reintroduced yourself to, "We are here for a shared purpose, and what I do is going to be benefited if you better understand it and can play a part in it." But that's where siloed leadership has gotten us. I have this conversation with CEOs all the time, and their big complaint is, "Claire, I can't get these guys and gals to collaborate, to work together. What's the secret?" So I ask, "How are you incentivizing them right now? Do they have shared objectives that are tied to compensation, or are they divided into 'Finance has their bucket' and 'Ops has their bucket' and sales and marketing and HR, and so on?" Again, you get that deer-in-the-headlights stare. Because they want collaboration, but they incentivize individual achievement. As long as those two things are in place at the same time, the money is going to win out— unless you have a unifying "why" that is authentically cascaded down to the point where you say, "This is what we are all pursuing. Yes, you have a finance leaning, and yes, you have a sales leaning, you have an operations leaning, or you're in a different geographic region, but we're all after this shared, unifying vision." Until those companies get there, the silos will perpetuate, and you will never grow, innovate and flog your competition to the level that you want.

❝Leaders want collaboration, but they incentivize individual achievement. As long as those two things are in place at the same time, the money is going to win out—unless you have a unifying why.❞

BB: Just think of the money it's costing organizations by the siloing. I'm sure at a certain size organization—and I'm sure it's not that big—it could be a million dollars, or it could be five million dollars, or it could be ten million dollars, through the inefficiencies that siloing causes and the animosity that it causes and the "us versus them," "my department versus your department," "my budget versus your budget," and "My project's more important than your project, so I'm going to sabotage your project so my project looks better and I look better to the CEO, and my fiefdom gets bigger than your fiefdom." When you look at companies that start looking that way—and I've seen them—I've sat in boardroom conversations where 15 people around a boardroom table really can't stand each other, because each one has competing agendas, and it's all about "my fiefdom." It's not about how we can make the company better; it's "How can I make sure that I get every single dime to fund the project that I want, my pet project?" That's when we start breaking down as organizations and asking, "Where's the focus?" The focus needs to be on the customer. End of story. You deal with your people, you deal with your purpose, and the profit comes. Your people are your internal people and your external people—they're all customers. They're all people who need to see the value in your brand and believe in your brand, see that they get value from the brand, and believe that they are being served by the brand. That needs to happen both internally and externally; those are your people. Then you need to have a strong purpose. If you can bring the people and the purpose together, the profit will come.

❝The focus needs to be on the customer. End of story. You deal with your people, you deal with your purpose, and the profit comes.❞

CC: Profit is a lagging indicator. It is not what should lead your decisions. it is the ultimate bottom-line scorecard, if you will. But instead of focusing on that first, ask, "How do we really unify this company and get them oriented collectively toward our why?" I've been in boardrooms, like you, where you can literally see the tension, you can see the seething anger, the discontent, the disconnect between the executives around the table. A lot of companies, by evolutionary design, have pitted their executives against each other, through their compensation, their view of power, the spoils of their individual wars. You talk about how this is costing money. The problem is that most companies can't quantify the opportunity cost. They can't quantify how much revenue or market share they DON'T have as a result of their lack of innovation. But the one big area where they CAN quantify—or the first big area, I should say, that they can quantify—opportunity costs, and I know this is right in your sweet spot, is the loss of well performing employees. You use the statistic all the time that every employee, regardless of level, costs a hundred thousand dollars to replace.

BB: Yes. And that's not an executive employee; an executive employee is two-and-a-half to three-and-a-half times your salary. The numbers are staggering. If you lose 10 employees a year, that's a million dollars off the bottom line.

CC: That's right. Even if you lose a mediocre performer—even if you lose a poor performer—if you are not unified around a very crystal-clear purpose, how do you know that the reason they were mediocre or subpar was because they didn't have the ability? How do you know it wasn't because you weren't guiding them in a way that they could clearly see the direction you're headed and how they contribute to it? Before you conduct your next scorecard evaluation—where you write the names of all the people on your team, and then label them as A players, B players and C players—you'd better make darn sure you've got rock-solid criteria against which you're evaluating their performance and their contribution. It's not bottom-line profit. It's how embedded they are in the organization, how well they manage their internal networks, how well they collaborate, and how well they contribute their individual strengths to the common purpose of the company.

BB: Forget everybody else; let's talk about sales. You got a guy or a girl who's been a top performer for a year, two years or five years, and all of a sudden they go into a slump, and all of a sudden two, three, four or five months go along, and they're not performing at the level that they were. The question should be, "Why?" Not, "It's time to get rid of this person," but "What's changed?" What are the challenges? Is there something that's keeping them from succeeding? Are there frustrations or roadblocks in the way? Is there a change in leadership? Are there things within the company that are making this person not as successful as they had been? Companies are great at saying, "Oh good, we got a great salesperson, they're doing really well; we're going to cut their territory in half, and we're going to double their quota." That is the classic thing that sales leaders do. Because we say, "We're going to get more out of them by giving them less." You wonder why they don't succeed. You wonder why they're frustrated. You wonder why great salespeople pick up, move to a different company, and take the customers with them. They may never contact those customers again, but those customers will find them. If there was a great sales rep, and that customer now feels that the new sales rep is not taking care of them, and they don't feel they're being taken care of the way they were by the sales rep that left, they're going to go looking to find out where that other person is. If that person is now somewhere else, and selling the same thing or selling something similar, I may move my business over there. Because that's where the relationship is; and with social media, those people are easy to find.

CC: That's exactly right. As you said earlier, people don't have relationships with companies; they have relationships with the people within them. This is a painful example right now, because we can't visit restaurants, but if you have a favorite local restaurant, you typically have a favorite bartender or a favorite waitstaff. You say, "Where's your zone today? Because I want to sit there." It's not because we think, "Well, nobody else can pour my wine the way that you can." We have a relationship; we have a rapport. As you talk about bringing this conversation internally, the notion that rotating, especially the C-Suite, through customer service—frequently, consistently, regularly, so that they can really have a first-hand account of the impact that not just their customer service reps, but everybody within the company, is having on the end goal, which is the customer—how powerful would it be for that same C-Suite to rotate through the employee base? To walk around, and ask those questions of a salesperson, to use that example, before they become a "problem employee"? To ask, "How are things going lately? How are you finding your job? Is there anything that is getting in your way of being ridiculously successful?" Because if you're ridiculously successful, yes, the company ultimately benefits from it, but you feel fulfilled as well. So how can we turn the light up in you to play to your strengths, to be in your zone, to get your feeling of self-worth as high as it can possibly be, so that you can deliver the best relationship to clients, prospects, customers and fellow employees that you can?

❝How can we turn the light up in you to play to your strengths, to be in your zone, to get your feeling of self-worth as high as it can possibly be, so that you can deliver the best relationship to clients, prospects, customers and fellow employees that you can?❞

BB: Here's the thing: Get over the ego. Because so many senior managers see salespeople who are making 250, 350, 550 thousand dollars a year, and they say, "Well, they can't make that much money; I'm not making that much money!" Well, guess what? Great salespeople are out there getting kicked in the teeth for the company every single day. They're the people who have the relationship with your customer. They're the ones doing that. If they're making 250, 350, 550 thousand dollars, then guess what? The company is making millions and millions of dollars. When I was working for a company, and I was head of the sales department, I had a hundred-million-dollar client. I was being paid very well to manage a hundred-million-dollar client; and most of it was bonus money. But guess what? My vice president was making good money, and so was the company; everybody was making profit based on the work that my salespeople and I were doing, because we were good at our jobs, and because we realized that, "If we can go out there and we can work harder, if we can build better customer relationships, if we can steal business away from our competitors because we're good at what we do, we're going to get compensated for it, and we're not going to get penalized because we made quota." There are a lot of people who do that: You make quota, and you're penalized because next year we're going to double your quota and cut your territory in half. All that does—and it doesn't matter if it's salespeople or marketing people or whatever—when you play with people's compensation, when you change the rules, when you upset the applecart, you better have a damn good reason why you're doing it, and explain why you're doing it before you go ahead and do it, so everybody's buying in. Because if they don't buy in, why should these people be loyal to you? Why should they be loyal to you as a leader? Why should they trust you? Why should they work for you? Why should they represent your company well, if you're not taking care of them?

❝If they don't buy in, why should employees be loyal to you? Why should they trust you?❞

CC: The biggest complaint I have heard from those who are the decision-makers in that compensation structure, and who reevaluate it or make an across-the-board cut—because "We've all got to cut back"—the biggest rebuttal they have to what you just said is, "Well, they have started to view this bonus, this commission, this long-term incentive, etc. as an entitlement. We're just not seeing the connection between that incentive and the output that we were hoping for, that we used to see." Again, I would argue that the compensation structure is a bit of a lagging indicator. You want to keep your employees motivated and reminded of your "why"; you want to keep them connected to how their personal role, their personal passions, and their unique strengths contribute to and move the needle toward the achievement of that why; and you want to keep them hungry. I don't mean starving, because you're paying them peanuts; I mean hungry in a sense that they are continually yearning, challenged, motivated and energized by contributing their very best relationships, talents and ideas to the collective good of the company.

BB: I absolutely agree. That comes down to everybody being on the same page. What is your why? What is your purpose? What is your purpose as an organization? Where are you going? Where are you today, where do you want to go, and is everybody on the bus with you? Because if your employees are not on the bus with you, your customers certainly won't be. We need to say, "We're heading to that mountain over there. That's what we want, the mountain we want to climb, and this is why we want to climb it, and this is what success we're going to get as a group because we climb that mountain. We're all going to be better off. Everybody on the bus? Great. Let's go."

CC: What happens when you get that type of clarity? You're going to find that some of the people that you called A players a week ago may not actually be A players. Or maybe they are, but they should be in a different role. So what ends up happening is you start with that mountaintop view, and you say, "This is where we're headed," then you say, "This is what we need." Not WHO we need, but WHAT we need to get there; these are the fundamental capabilities, the fundamental attributes we must have as an organization, in our DNA, to get there. Okay, great. Now, who do we have on the team already, which of those fundamental attributes do they already have, and what's the gap? Now you've got a tangible target, a common enemy, that you can address, versus arbitrarily calling Joe an A player and Jill a C player, because of their performance based on fuzzy descriptions of what their role should be, and fuzzy paths toward a future that has not been clearly defined.

BB: For every company today, now is the perfect time to be leveling up: to be able to look at your people and say, "Over the last however many number of weeks or months, who stepped up and who stepped back?" Take a really clear look and say, "Who are the people who were on board? Who are the people who were on the team? Who are the people who were willing to drive the bus?" Those people need to be rewarded for their loyalty, their hard work, their dedication, and the challenges that they've gone through. But we also need to look at the people and say, "Who are the people who've just sat on their couch and ate bonbons for the last six months, and really didn't get their job done, and made excuse after excuse after excuse?" Whether they're leadership, frontline managers, or employees, take a look and say, "Did these people hold their weight?" You're going to have circumstances—for instance, I was dealing with someone, she was a single mom of four young kids, recently divorced, lived in 650 square feet; really difficult for her to do her job well from home with no help—so we need to take those things into consideration. But if we truly have people who have literally sat on their behinds and used every excuse—"Well, it's COVID season; we don't have to do anything because we can get away with anything"—those are the people we need to look at and say, "Are those the people we want on the bus long term?" Be able to have the hard conversations with those people and say, "We're disappointed in what you've done. This is what we need; this is what we're expecting moving forward. Is this something that you're capable of?" You're right: It comes down to a clear definition of roles, of purpose. Because we're in a world where virtual is reality: We can have a team in Oklahoma; we can have a team in Nebraska; we can have a team in Alaska; we can have a team in Texas; we can have a team in Toronto or Vancouver. We can have teams where we need them, or people where we need them, to be able to be effective and use technology in a way that allows us to engage these people and get the best people where they are—instead of having to motivate them and pay them twenty thousand dollars to move to a different city, away from their family or whatever. Let them be where they are, let them be successful in the communities that they like to be in, and still be productive, contributing members of your company. So now is the time we need to start thinking about leveling up our companies and say, "All right; in the United States, there are 40 million people on unemployment insurance. Who are the good catches? Who are the people we should be looking at and saying, 'How can we fill the roles that we know we need moving forward, and not worry about whether they can come into the office 9:00 to 5:00, Monday to Friday?'" Find out if these are the people that can help us get where we need to go and give us the toolset that we don't already have, to be able to serve our customers better.

> **❝It comes down to a clear definition of roles, of purpose.❞**

CC: That 9:00 to 5:00 expectation is dead for an overwhelming majority of roles now. We've proven that through this forced pivot. There are always going to be essential employees in roles that cannot make that pivot, who have to work on site, not just to get their job done but to get our customers' needs met. But a couple of things come up for me in what you just said. We talked about "What are the fundamental attributes that your company will need, that are specific to the DNA that is going to be required to get your mission achieved?" Those are going to be unique from company to company, industry to industry. But two of those attributes, coming through this pandemic, have become mission-critical for any company, of any size, in any industry: resilience and adaptability. You talked about how there are certain people throughout the ranks—from C-Suite on down—who have used COVID-19 as an excuse to coast. There are certain employees who get a pass because they were juggling some other things. But I had this same conversation with somebody recently, and he said, "Some businesses are not ready to look ahead yet. They're just trying to survive through this." I understand that, but the very top leadership, must have one eye on getting their business through the crisis, while keeping the other eye on that horizon. They have no choice. As we've talked about, the companies that will not get through this are the companies that can't see that, that cannot figure out how to—not do business as usual—do business in this new normal. Not just focus on getting the lights back on. It really brings up, as you just said, the phrase "this excuse of COVID." It's not like my business just burned down because of the carelessness of the guy who owns the restaurant next door to me, and so I have a very localized crisis that you all need to give me a pass on. This is a globally shared crisis. You cannot use COVID-19 as an excuse to ignore or mistreat or sub-serve your customers or your employees. You just can't do it. As we know, the reality is not all businesses are going to get through this. But even if you are a business that will ultimately fail, until the very last day that you turn the lights out for good, make sure you treat your employees and your customers like the family that you want to have in that relationship. Because that's what they're going to remember. That's going to be your legacy. Even if you were the head of an ultimately failed business, they're going to remember how you treated them.

❝Two of those attributes, coming through this pandemic, have become mission-critical for any company, of any size, in any industry: resilience and adaptability.❞

BB: As Maya Angelou said, it's not what you said, it's not what you did, it's how you made people feel. That goes with people inside and outside the company; it doesn't really matter. People want to feel listened to, understood and valued. It comes down to that. If we can listen to, understand and value both employees and customers, and understand that we are nothing without them, and in our role as leaders every day wake up and say, "How can we make people's lives better around us?" If we can wake up every morning and ask, "What do we need to do to build better tools to allow other people to succeed around us?" Those are the companies that are going to go far. You're absolutely correct: We all need to have one eye on the horizon. The conversations I'm having right now, I'm starting to do a lot of roundtables with customers about what's next. Assessing what has happened, where we are and where we want to be. What policies and procedures happened during the crisis that were Band-Aid solutions that were relevant during the time of crisis, but no longer relevant and no longer need to be a de facto policy or procedure? What needs to change? What are the elephants in the room that need to be discussed? What cows need to be killed? Because there are no sacred cows anymore. In order to move the business forward, we need to be able to say, "Where do we want to be?" Every business has an opportunity right now to have a clean slate and say, "Who do we want to be moving forward?" Because this is global. Everybody's affected. Everybody is in a position where they're moving forward from a step backwards. And because of that, we as organizations need to be asking, "Who are the people we truly want to serve? What is our true value in the world? Who are we valuable to? Why are we valuable to them? What do we do that makes people's lives better?" And make sure that not only our customers know this, but our employees know this. Because if they understand where we're going, and how they belong to that, and how what they do matters, and they're empowered to help the customers achieve their goals, they're going to be more engaged, stay longer, become better advocates for the brand, and build better customer experience and more loyal clients. And guess what? Those customers are going to be less price-sensitive. So, we need to start thinking that way. As leaders, we need to start thinking, "What's the experience that we want to have moving forward?" We need to be able to empower that experience both inside and outside our corporations, to be able to say, "Our client base may be smaller, but that client base that we have is way more loyal and way more valuable to us."

❝Every business has an opportunity right now to have a clean slate and say, "Who do we want to be moving forward?"❞

CC: True, authentic, genuine relationships build loyalty; and the loyalty is what builds profitability.

QUESTION:

How do you define customer experience within your organization? What are you doing to ensure that your customer receives the same experience at every touchpoint?

_____

_____

_____

_____

_____

_____

_____

_____

_____

EPISODE 10

THE SPRINT VS. THE MARATHON MENTALLY

BB: Let's talk about sprint vs. marathon mentality. This is something leaders really need to be looking at: Are we constantly in sprint mode? Or are we saying, "There are certain things that we need to be sprinting towards; however, most situations require us to be in marathon mode." I want to dive into that. So Claire, I want your initial thoughts on this, and then we can dive into this together.

CC: It's such an important topic. Throughout this conversation series, we have been emphasizing that leaders— smart leaders and smart companies—are keeping one eye on crisis mode, because we cannot overlook or underestimate this common global enemy of COVID-19. But we also have to maintain our other eye on the horizon and play for the longer game, which is so fitting for your analogy of the marathon mentality. You already have raised a good point, that it's not an either/or; it's not a black-or-white situation. There are a lot of things in leadership, in running a company, in going beyond just keeping the lights on, that have to do with sprints. There are certain things that speak to the agility of a company. So companies need to be agile; they need to be able to make decisions quickly, but not hastily, and always keep an eye on the long game. I think this is such an important topic for us to dive into.

❝Companies need to be agile; they need to be able to make decisions quickly, but not hastily, and always keep an eye on the long game.❞

BB: I agree with you. Because it's not just today; it's moving forward for the next 5, 10, 15, 20 years—or towards the next hundred years. We're always going to have crises. There may not be a worldwide crisis—it may be a crisis within the organization; it could be something that just happened today—but if we're constantly living in crisis mode, if we're constantly living in sprint mode, if we're constantly saying, "We're going to be the duck, where we look calm on the very top but we're paddling like mad underneath," that really creates a horrible place for companies to be mentally. It stresses people out if they are constantly saying, "I have to do this, and then I have to do this," and they're always thinking, "When am I going to be able to catch my breath? We're always running at a million miles an hour." I remember years ago being in the ad agency business, and everything was a sprint; everything was a crisis; everything was last-minute; everything was all-nighters to make an 8 o'clock in the morning presentation. You're printing something on the color printer at 5 o'clock in the morning and binding it up and rushing to a client's office at 8 a.m., hoping there are no spelling mistakes, hoping you caught everything. Then the next day, you got up and you did it all over again. What does that do? That creates ulcers. That creates unnecessary stress. It creates an environment where you do get those creative juices going, but you also get a lot of burnout. That's burnout from the staff, burnout from the leaders, and burnout from senior management. Where you're always going in sprint mode, always going at a million miles an hour just trying to catch up, huge mistakes happen, and employee churn is normal. What if instead, we set our eyes on the horizon and ask, "Where are we going? Where do we want to be? Where do we want to be five years from now? 10 years from now? 20 years from now?" We know that's going to change. Nobody has the perfect crystal ball; no one's got the understanding that we're going to make a five-year plan and things are going to go exactly to plan. They're not. Things are going to hit you; you're going to have to go into crisis mode; you're going to have to go into sprint mode every once in a while. You're going to have to take three steps back, you're going to have to punt, you're going to have employee changes, customer changes, etc. Things happen. But if we have an eye on the goal, if we keep an eye on the horizon, if we're always saying, "This is where we want to go," we start looking at things with a different vision, with a different viewpoint. I think leaders need to start thinking that way: Instead of managing from crisis to crisis leaders start saying to their people, "We trust you to get stuff done. This is where we're going; this is what we're doing." We need to start running the business with this viewpoint in mind, with thinking and acting long-term. Leaders need to ask, "What's our vision for this customer for the next five or ten years?" not "What's the customer vision with this customer for the next 30 days?" That's the mentality shift that we need to start thinking about for customers if we're going to be successful—forget whether it's COVID-19; forget whether it's this crisis or another—whether we're going to be successful as corporations moving forward.

❝We're always going to have crises.… But if we're constantly living in crisis mode, if we're constantly living in sprint mode… that really creates a horrible place for companies to be mentally.❞

CC: That's so true. There is such a key difference between agility and firefighting. There's a difference between strategic crisis management and haphazard management by chaos. We talked about this on one of our previous episodes: How many leaders do we know who thrive in chaos? They thrive when there are a hundred spinning plates, and there's all this ambiguity and uncertainty. Business will always have ambiguity. And things will change. You can have a very long-term view—you can have a strategic plan and a roadmap to get there—but there will always be the need for course corrections. Companies need to have a clearer eye toward where they want to get to—not end up, but strive toward— because if they do, they will have a much easier time adjusting to those bumps in the road or those major hills like we're going through with COVID-19. The other thing you talked about is burnout. Leaders may thrive in chaos, but they must constantly be mindful of the impact they have on their people. They need to be aspiring—all of us, as leaders, need to be aspiring—to make as positive and forward-moving an impact as we can on the people we lead and the people who follow us. But those who manage by chaos—as their normal, standard operating procedure; their normal, standard playbook—the burnout risk is so high. You're sending a message—not that you're agile, or that you're flexible, or that you're spontaneous—but that you don't know what the hell you're doing.

❝There's a difference between strategic crisis management and haphazard management by chaos.❞

BB: It's that chaos that leads to culture burnout. If everybody in the office is looking at you asking, "What are you doing? Why didn't you anticipate this? Why weren't you thinking five steps ahead? Why are we in this situation AGAIN?" If that is what they are thinking, why would your team trust you? Why would your team pick up their axes and hoses and run into the fire with you? If every single day they're picking up their axes and hoses they're running right into another fire, eventually they are going to start running the other way. They'll go into the fire once; they'll go into the fire twice; they might even go into the fire three times, if it's an exception and not a rule. If they believe the person leading them is not constantly sending them towards another burning building. Because you can get totally and absolutely burned out if you're just living in a constant state of chaos. If you, as an employee, are constantly asking, "Where are we going now? We made this plan, we said we were going in this direction, and then all of a sudden we're moving over here, and then we're moving over there, and then we're moving over here again." How does that affect you as someone being led? It leads to employees thinking, "Forget it. I'm done! I'm going somewhere else." Every employee who leaves you costs $100,000 to replace. So why would you want to lead through chaos? Why would you want to be constantly in sprint mode and not building the trust of people, not giving them the vision and the direction and the leadership that they deserve, so that they can trust you, so when the sprint needs to happen, they're saying, "This is an exception; this is not a rule. This is okay. The stuff has hit the fan. We need to take care of it. All hands on deck. We need to take care of this. Something unexpected happened. It's nobody's fault. Let's go." That's a completely different thought process than, "Here we go again." I think that, as leadership, we need to say, "What is the message that's going on in everybody's mind, when we all of a sudden hit the panic button?"

❝Why would you want to constantly be in sprint mode and not building the trust of people, not giving them the vision and the direction and the leadership that they deserve, so that they can trust you?❞

CC: I have to laugh because I know a lot of leaders who thrive in chaos, and they wear that proudly: "I manage by chaos." Their justification for it is, "We're an entrepreneurial culture." "Entrepreneurial" doesn't mean you're making it up as you go; entrepreneurial <u>does</u> mean you are agile, maybe you're not as weighed down by bureaucracy, but it doesn't mean you don't have a plan. Entrepreneurial should mean "I know where I want us to go, and we're not going to take the typical corporate path that's weighed down by a lot of approval gates, but we still have a master plan." I'm reminded of the great conversation we had about the customer experience. One of the things that we talked about was that the businesses and the brands that rise above everyone else—because everyone makes mistakes—are the companies and the entities that know how to recover. So your analogy of going in and fighting a fire repeatedly: If there are different fires for different reasons, that's one thing. If you give people the tools to fight that fire head-on—versus by blind luck they made it through alive—it's then incumbent upon good companies and good leaders, after the dust has settled and the smoke has cleared, to say, "How are we going to recover from this? What will we learn from this? How will we get stronger? What will we put in place, to shore up our technical infrastructure and evolve as a learning organization, to ensure that we never repeat the same mistakes?"

BB: If you're doing the same thing over and over again expecting different results, that's the definition of insanity. People MANAGE by crisis, but they LEAD people into the future. That management by crisis, as you said, is without a plan. It's by the seat of your pants. We woke up this morning, and the phone rang, and my entire world has to change. But does it? Does somebody else's sense of panic change YOUR sense of reality? Do you have to jump every time somebody screams? Do you have to say, "This is a 9-1-1 for somebody else, so it becomes a 9-1-1 for me, and therefore it becomes a 9-1-1 for my people"? Well, wait a second here. Let's sit down and talk about it. The first thing leaders need to do when they pick up the phone is say, "How much of a 9-1-1 is this?" How many things in our life are truly life-and-death? How many things are truly 9-1-1? Now, there absolutely are some. Perfect example: A number of years ago, I was in Hawaii, actually driving up Haleakala, in Maui, driving up the mountain, and my phone rang. It was a client. He said, "Where are you?" I said, "You don't really want to know." He said, "No, seriously, where are you?" I said, "Before I answer this, you need to realize my wife and my six-year-old kid are in the car." "Okay." I said, "I'm on Maui; I'm up at 8,000 feet, on my way up to Haleakala. How can I help you?" Then I heard this *bleep* at the other end of the phone. I asked, "What's wrong? Hang on; let me pull over." So I pulled over and had a quick conversation with this guy; there was a rules and regulation change that meant that he needed to get a quarter million pieces of direct mail out to his clients by January 5th, and this was over Christmas. So I said, "Look. It's early in the morning here. We're heading up the mountain. I'll be back in two hours. In two hours and five minutes, I will be on the phone with you, and we will figure this out." And we did. It wasn't cheap, but we got it done; we pulled a team together, and we organized it. But the reason I was able to pull a team together over Christmas—not only to design this thing, but to print the materials and the envelopes, get it into the direct mail, and out to the customers in time—was because I had built up a level of trust, not only with the customer, but with the sub-trades that I used to make this thing happen. We need to ask, "What is the issue? What is the problem? When does this need to be done?" Is this like "If you don't stop the car and turn around right now, and we deal with this right now, my life is going to come to an end"? Or

"Can I call you in two hours? Can I have some time to think about this, figure out what I need to do, and then give you a call?" That goes inside the company; it goes outside the company. That's the mentality that we need to have, to be able to assess, "Are we going into sprint mode, or is this just another mile on the marathon that we just need to figure out how to get over that hill?"

❝People MANAGE by crisis, but they LEAD people into the future.❞

CC: There's so much to unpack in that story. First, are we sprinting just because that is our muscle memory, that is our habit not to stop and say, "Is this truly something we need to sprint toward?" Or is this something we can take a little bit more time with? Don't get me started about the ubiquitous cell phone—kudos to Hawaii for having such a great cell signal when you're 8,000 feet up a mountain—but that's the other thing: We are never truly disconnected from our customers, from our business. There's a positive to that, but there's a negative too. The negative, of course, is you can never fully let go and get that perspective and work on your own sanity and your own burnout prevention program. But the good side is that there is that connection. Your clients know that they can rely on you. One of the things in our business, not just as leaders, but as guides to leadership—and it's a lesson for business leaders as well—is to be a voice of reason amidst the chaos, not the cause of or the furtherance of that chaos. So, in that example, where the client contacted you and said, "The world's on fire," you had the wherewithal to say, "Let's evaluate: Is this a five-alarm fire, or is this contained within a dust bin that we can put a lid on?" Providing that voice of calm—even though it did turn out to be a little bit of a crisis that you had to manage through—you were able to get him to exhale. Part of the job of any good leader is not just to give their employees space to breathe and figure things out on their own and come up with great ideas and new ways of doing things that perhaps they haven't thought about, but also to give them the peace of mind to exhale. You talked about this: Why is it that, every time, we go down to the wire, and we're working all-nighters? Well, why do women get bigger and bigger purses? Why do we constantly move into homes that have more and more closet space? The first thing we say is, "I could never possibly fill that space." Well, hold my beer. We expand to fit the space that we are provided. That is just as true when it comes to time. If we're given 27 days to put together a proposal or a marketing brochure or a strategic plan, we take 26 and a half days, and we go right up until the FedEx or delivery deadline. Because we think, "Well, we've been given this time, so we should fill this time." That's a sprinting mentality. Contrast that with a marathon mentality, which asks, "Where do we want to be on day 27? What is the image we want to present? What is the message we want to deliver through this plan, this proposal, this event?" Use that as your guidance, as your GPS, to say, "Yes, there will be gates, and we're going to need to sprint between some of those gates; but we are going to take measured steps through the others." If you're doing this the right way, and you're playing the long game, you're going to be taking more measured steps—and reevaluating and recovering when necessary—than you are sprinting from gate to gate.

❝Be a voice of reason amidst the chaos, not the cause of or the furtherance of that chaos.❞

BB: We need to look at the world in a marathon mentality, and give our employees the opportunity to look at the world in that the same way: Not everything is a crisis, and everything and anything can be planned out. If it can't be planned out in the long term, it can be planned out in the short term. Even in that crisis mode, even in that sprint mentality, we need to start thinking, "What's the end goal? What's the end game? What are we trying to achieve? What are we really trying to achieve?" It's not just getting this proposal out the door; it's about understanding what getting this proposal out the door is going to do. Or by spending all night doing this, how does this further not only the company's objectives; how do we take care of our customer, and what is this going to do for the team? That's what leaders need to be thinking about: It's the why. It's not the what, it's not the how; it's the why.

QUESTION:

What are the sprint decisions you have made, and are continuing to make? Are they still applicable as you move towards a marathon mentality?

_____

_____

_____

_____

_____

_____

_____

_____

_____

EPISODE 11

COMMUNICATION VS. CONNECTION

CC: I want to bring us back to the story of you in Hawaii. You told a story of being on a Christmas break, on a holiday with your family in Hawaii, and a client called as you were at 8,000 feet above sea level, and only halfway up your climb. You had to take a pause from your family vacation to deal with a client. So, one, I was super-jealous because I haven't been to Hawaii yet. But I also wanted to revisit the importance of not just being a voice of reason in a sea of chaos, but also this goodwill, this equity that you build up with a client over time, so that you can push back, manage expectations, say, "How big of a fire is this, really?" and "We're in this together." You talked about understanding the need for both communication and connection. I really wanted us to unpack that in this episode, because there is a significant difference between communicating and connecting. A lot of leaders screw that up; they think that they've reached out, they've had a town hall, or they've sent out a memo, or they've walked around and talked to employees or their senior leadership team—and all that's great, people who are doing that should continue to do that, because communication is absolutely critical—but they confuse it with connecting. Communication requires and implies that you've got a sender of a message and a receiver of the message. So even though we talk this good game about two-way communication, it's always one way at a time. Connection is much deeper than that. It's genuine. It's intimate in the sense that when you connect personally and deeply with an employee, as a leader, that's really where the engagement starts to come in. That's what you build culture on. You don't build culture on messages; you build culture on meaning. Real meaning is established through connection, not through communications. So I want to get your reaction and have you build on that.

❝You don't build culture on messages; you build culture on meaning. Real meaning is established through connection, not through communications.❞

BB: I agree with you. There's one-way communication, and there's two-way communication—which is really what we need. You need to be able to say something, but you also need to make sure that the person you're talking to hears it, understands it, and values it. Because if people value what you have to say, they're going to internalize it; and if they internalize it, it becomes part of THEIR reality, and now you have buy-in from them. That's the emotional connection. The emotional connection is built on trust. Trust is hard to get, it's easy to lose, and it's almost impossible to get back. We spend a lifetime saying, "Why don't they trust me?" Well, people don't trust you because you're not trustworthy. That's not a slight; it's more of a fact that you need to ask, "What have you done to deserve their trust?" Just because you're their boss—just because you have a position of power over people in one way, shape or form—doesn't mean they should trust you. They may work for you; they may do things for you based on the fact that they're getting paid for it or, if they don't do it, there are ramifications. But none of that has to do with connection. None of that has anything to do with trust. The people who stick around month after month, year after year, decade after decade do so because they trust the company, the value of the company, and understand the why of the company. Not only that, they believe that the corporate why is their why as well and they trust the people in the company to know that they're doing things in their best interest as employees. That's really important; it's building those connections between employees and leaders and that develops trust. As I said about running into the fire: We'll run into the fire for somebody we trust; we'll run into fires for somebody we're connected to, somebody that we have an emotional connection with, somebody that we can say, "They would do the same for me, so off we go." But if there isn't that emotional connection, if there isn't that resonance to go along with it, there is no trust; there is no connection. We need to start thinking about that as leaders: "Why do people follow me? Do they follow me because they're afraid of me, because they're being paid to do it, because if they don't do it their spouse and their kids may not eat or they might be out of work?" Or do they do it because they say, "I believe in the person who is my boss, who is my leader, who is the person that I report to, because I know that they're going to take care of me, and I know that I understand what the mission, vision and values are, what the brand story is, and that it matters to me, because I can see that I'm part of the future of the company. I trust that if I take care of them, they're going to take care of me." So I'm with you 100 percent: Connection, trust, culture... they're all intertwined. That's what leadership is truly all about.

❝Connection, trust, culture... they're all intertwined. That's what leadership is truly all about.❞

CC: In all of what you just described, as well, is loyalty. There's a difference between merely being satisfied— which, again, is important, and we measure it, and there are plenty of vendors and plenty of surveys out there that will help you measure the satisfaction of your employees—but satisfaction only goes so far, which is why we started to talk in terms of engagement. But really what you're getting down to is loyalty. True loyalty can't be adequately measured by a survey tool, and it cannot be built by even the most cleverly crafted communication. Communication has to be genuine; it has to be authentic. When it's done right, when it's done in those ways, it does build connection. You can have a one-way communication that you've convinced yourself is two-way, but a connection has to be mutually agreed-upon; it has to be mutually felt. Otherwise there is no connection. So that's one of the reasons that we talk so much about the value of a brand story. The true brand story of these forward-looking companies shows how I as an individual employee connect in some way, in some sense, to the company. That connection is not built through compensation; it's not built through fear of the boss I report to, or fear of being put out into the unemployment market. It is built through "I feel a genuine connection between my core why, my core purpose, where I feel I can bring the most value to an employer, and how that feeds the company's mission." And vice versa: "I can see how, the farther along we are toward the company's vision, the more that feeds my own why." So that's why connection is so much deeper than communication—and heavily relies on communication— but it's so much deeper, because it is truly that two-way, mutually built up, mutually maintained and sustained relationship.

❝Connection is so much deeper than communication... because it is truly that two-way, mutually built up, mutually maintained and sustained relationship.❞

BB: You bring up the whole idea of surveys, 360s, evaluations, etc. The problem with all those is that they are one-way communications. Most employee evaluations or 360s obtain information in one direction. It's one-way communication: "I want to tell you how I think about you, and that's it," or "I'm trying to get information from you." But there's no two-way communication with that. That's why a lot of the stuff breaks down. Everybody sees wonderful engagement surveys: "How engaged do you feel in the office? 5%, 10%, 20%, 30%, 40%?" Does that really tell the story that you want to know? Does it really make your employees feel valued by taking these surveys? Are they answering them realistically? Are they answering them honestly? Based on the fact they're going to say, "What's the hidden agenda?" A lot of people think of that. People say, "First of all, I don't have the time," or "I don't want to make the time to do this," or "If, to be 100% compliant, I have to do this, I'm just going to tick boxes." What does any company learn from that? But when you have that two-way dialogue, when you have that connection, when you have that story, then it's not about you. It's about, "How do we interact?" and "How do we engage together?" That's the thing with leadership. Leadership has to forget about the ego and say, "What could I be doing better?" and actually ask employees, "How can I serve YOU better?" Put the ego aside and actually listen to what they have to say. You may not be able to do everything they want to do, you may not be perfect, and there may be things that you just can't change. But the simple act of actually listening to people, taking notes, and being actively engaged in the conversation builds that connection. You may say, "Listen. I can do this, I can do this, but that is completely out of my control. I can try going to bat for you—in fact, I WILL go to bat for you—and let's see what we can do. Maybe we can come up with a compromise." Then get back to them and say, "Look. I talked to senior management. We can't do this; we just don't have the budget. We don't have the bandwidth to implement this right now, but we can do this as a pilot program. Would you be interested in helping me run the pilot program, to be able to see where this goes from here? Then maybe next year, if this thing goes well, we can build it into the budget." Think of the connection that you just built with that employee, by having that open and honest two-way conversation and saying, "We can't do this now, but what we can do is a small pilot, figure out if this is going to work, try it out, experiment on a small level, and if this works, we can allocate budget to it in the next fiscal year." You haven't blown people off; you've found a different way of dealing with a situation which is not a no, but it's not a yes either. You can do it in such a way that it's a win for everybody: Everybody feels that they've been listened to, understood and valued. You built a connection. You built trust. You built a relationship. All of a sudden, an employee says, "They went to bat for me. They actually took my idea and ran it up the ladder and gave me credit for it. They didn't take and make it their own suggestion." That person's going to turn around and tell every other employee, "The company is letting me do this. Do you want to get involved?" All of a sudden, you build that relationship up within the company, and people believe that senior management is listening, that change is possible, that my opinion and my thoughts and my ideas matter. And that's how connection is built. Not through a 360, not through a quarterly review, not through a survey that's done through a third-party company. It's by actual communication and conversation.

❝That's how connection is built.... It's by actual communication and conversation.❞

CC: Now think about the power of that feedback loop that got created through that example. It started with a conversation. It started with creating that environment, so we can have that kind of dialogue, and then listening intently. You didn't say the word "why," but it was implied in everything that you took us through, with that example of "Some things I'll be able to implement or approve right away; some are a hard no; some we're going to have to run up the chain, but I'm going to come back to you, we're going to talk again, and you're going to know why or why not." Because it ties to the mission, or it's just not something we can fund right now, or what have you. Surveys don't work because of everything you outlined. If you sit down with your leader—your direct manager—and they start that conversation with, "What could we be doing differently, better, etc. that will make your job better, make this process easier, make you more productive?" versus saying, "You probably saw that email from HR; make sure you finish the survey before the end of the week, and we're going to see what kind of results we get." It's so disconnected. The first thing that employees ask themselves and ask you—not out loud, but through their behavior—when they get an invitation to take a satisfaction survey is, "What's in it for me?" If you've done surveys in the past, you probably didn't do a great job of communicating back the results, AND what you intended to do with those results. So you've already chipped away at people's willingness to even participate in this survey, let alone be honest and constructive. The other thing that surveys just don't get right, but that the feedback loop you outlined really underscores, is that people support what they help to create. The fastest way to get buy-in from employees on something you want to implement is to ask them for their ideas. Even if you don't implement them wholesale, make that connection— there's that word again—back to whatever you do as a company, and whatever decisions senior leadership makes. Always tie it back to something the employees expressed as an idea a need, or a concern. That's how you build connection, and that's how you foster loyalty.

Loyalty and connection are what make companies sustainable, profitable and successful.

> **❝Loyalty and connection are what make companies sustainable, profitable and successful.❞**

BB: I agree. How many times have surveys gone out, and are filled out, and then nothing happens?

CC: They get lost in the ether.

BB: You get no feedback loop, there is no change implemented within the company, you don't even know if anybody actually read it, and all it becomes is a dashboard, a check mark that says, "We sent out a satisfaction survey, that goes on the HR report. Good. We've done our duty." All you're doing by doing that is ticking people off. The only thing you're doing by sending out those obligatory quarterly employee satisfaction surveys is ticking people off, if you're not willing to honestly read through every single comment, amalgamate the data, have a conversation about it, say, "This, this and this are coming up over and over again; we need to change these things," then put the time, the money, the energy, and the effort into making that happen. Say, "We've listened to you. You said that this, this and this were major problems. We hear you. These are the things that we're working on. We're going to come back to you within the next 90 days with a solution to fix this. By the way, we'd like to have some key employees sit on this committee to make sure we get it right; who wants to volunteer?" That's how you build a connection. That's how you get people excited. They get involved, and they feel that they've been heard, that they've been valued, that they've been listened to. These are huge things that most companies just tick a box, because it looks good on some survey somewhere.

❝That's how you get people excited. They get involved, and they feel that they've been heard, that they've been valued, that they've been listened to.❞

CC: You used the word "compliance" earlier. If you're only doing that to comply with what they see as—and communicate to their employees as—an HR exercise, it's a waste of time, money, and the human capital that you have in your team. If a survey—annually, quarterly or otherwise—is the only time you, as a leader, are asking for input from your employees, then you're not a leader, and you're not doing it right.

BB: That is an incredible place to finish this. If you're not waking up every single morning as a leader and saying, "How can I make my team better? How can I engage them? How can I make sure that they're passionate? How can I give them the tools that they need to succeed? How do we develop trust? How do we further the conversation in such a way that everybody understands the mission, vision and values, the brand story, and believes that it matters to them?" then you're not doing your job as a leader. Plain and simple.

QUESTION:

How do you know that the vital messages you want to communicate will be received, understood, internalized and acted upon?

_____

_____

_____

_____

_____

_____

_____

_____

_____

EPISODE 12

REVERTING VS. REINVENTING

BB: I'm excited, because this is something that really ties a bow around everything that we've talked about. Let's talk about reverting versus reinventing. I talked a few weeks ago about re-onboarding, that every single employee is going to need to be re-onboarded, because there are going to be changes in every company. We need to think, "Are we going to revert to where we were? Or are we going to take the time and reinvent and make ourselves better?" So I want your thoughts on this, Claire, because this is something that you're absolutely passionate about.

CC: I have this super-clear visual in my head of a tunnel. If you've ever driven into a major city—whether it's New York City, or Toronto, or Seattle, or LA, or any of these major cities—and you have to go through a tunnel, you'd better know where you're going by the time you get out of that tunnel. Because as soon as you see the light at the end that signals that you're out of the tunnel, you have to make a very quick decision. In a lot of cases, it's a quick left or it's a quick right. You can't get to the end of the tunnel, stop, weigh your options, and then make a decision after careful deliberation. Because—especially in New York—you're going to have a boatload of cars behind you laying on their horns. I'm from New Jersey, where the car horn is a natural extension of our hand; we don't distinguish them as two different things. So you're going to lay on the horn, and you're going to say, "Hey, buddy, where are you going? Make a decision!" So before you even get to that tunnel, you'd better know that you're going to have to make a decision at the end of it, and you'd better know which way you're supposed to go. So, translating that into business, those people honking the horns behind you are your people. We are starting to see the light at the end of the tunnel; we have started to see the economy reopening from this pandemic. As leaders, we are starting to say, "We're still keeping an eye on that, and the impact it has on our business, but we really need to move forward." So when you look at that light at the end of this tunnel, you've got a very clear decision to make. You just outlined those two options very clearly: We can revert back to business as usual, the "old normal"; or we can reinvent who we are, what we're about, why we're in existence, where we're going to go, and how we're going to get there. So it's such a clear visual for me. And I have horrible flashbacks of my first time driving into New York City, because it is a very harrowing experience; and the people behind you are very unforgiving if you don't know what you're doing.

66When you look at that light at the end of this tunnel, you've got a very clear decision to make. 99

BB: I love the visual. You don't have time to hesitate when you come out of the tunnel. You're right. As somebody who has driven around the world—I've lived in Israel, I've lived in New York City, I've actually lived in Toronto and

LA as well—drivers are unforgiving. They know where they're going; they expect you to know where you're going too. If you don't, they're going to let you know. So you need to—right now, right this very moment, and quite honestly as long as your business exists—say, "Are we going to revert to what we've always done? Or can we take the time to evaluate what's working, what isn't working, who are we doing it for? What policies and procedures do we have? Are there any sacred cows?" Are there things that we should be asking, "Why are we still doing this?" or "Why are we still dealing with this customer?" or "Why do we still have this policy?" We need to be critical of things as we move forward. Because we're human beings: We change; we evolve; our businesses change; our customers change; the market changes; the world changes. Why are we as businesses not changing? Why are we not taking the time right now to say, "What has changed? What's better? What's different? What things did we do in 9-1-1 mode, back when we were in the sprint mode? What were the decisions that we made, the policies and procedures that got us through that sprint mode? Now that we're back in marathon mode, are those still relevant? Why are we still doing these? Why do we still have these on the books? Why are we still operating in sprint mode, when we should be operating in marathon mode?" Look at your customers and say, "We've got 5,000, 10,000, 15,000 customers— or even 20, 50, or 100 customers—which are the ones who serve us best? Which ones are we not adding value to? Which ones are taking up way too much time for the value that they're providing us in terms of dollars and cents?" Take a look at it not only from a dollar and cents point of view, but is this a customer that we don't do a lot of work with, but who refers a ton of business to us? We need to be questioning it on a person-by-person, a step-by-step, a policy-by-policy basis, to say, "How can we be better?" This set of decisions can't just happen in an ivory tower, around a boardroom table, away from everything. We need to talk to our customers; we need to talk to our employees; we need to look at the policies. We need to figure out what's on the books. What are the laws of the companies that are no longer relevant, and why are we still abiding by them? Has our brand changed? Has our culture changed? Has our purpose changed? We need to be able to say, "What does this mean to us as a company?" Talk to our employees and say, "What are we doing as a company that you really like? What are the things that you see that are inefficient?" It could be the way that we deal with customers; it could be the fact that employees don't feel empowered, that they don't feel that the current methods of communication are effective; it could be one of a million different things. But we need to talk to our people and say, "There are no sacred cows, there is nothing on the books that can't be discussed." Let's talk about it as a company and say, "Is this working? Yes. Could this work better? Yes. How? Why? Great; let's move forward. Is this working? No. Then why are we doing it?" There might be a reason why you still do it. But if you don't ask, "Why are we doing this?" and "Is this holding us back?" you're never going to be able to reinvent yourself.

"If you don't ask, "Why are we doing this?" and "Is this holding us back?" you're never going to be able to reinvent yourself."

CC: I can think of very few companies right now that have gotten through this pandemic without cutting back people, whether it's laying off a bunch of people, or putting them on furlough, or making the very difficult decision to shut down divisions or offices, etc., for the sake of pruning, so that the entire tree does not die. Those employees who are still with you, and the customers who stuck with you through this, there's a loyalty there that you need to capitalize on. But you need to do it in genuine ways. We've talked a lot about the importance of connection, and the importance of having feedback loops and genuine dialogue with your people, where they feel listened to, understood and valued. We ended our last episode with a little bit of tough love. I have some tough love for the C-Suite in particular, but also anyone who is a leader right now: Take the phrase "Because of this pandemic, we need to do more with less" OUT of your vocabulary. If any of you come out of this, and your message to the people who have stuck by you and the customers who have stuck by you is, "We have fewer resources, but the workload remains, and we have to do more with less," shame on you. Because there is NO time that that message lands well with employees; but particularly coming out of a pandemic that has affected every one of us professionally and personally, it will not resonate AT ALL. I understand that the underlying business message may be that you will have to do as much or more than you did before, but your resources are more constrained. Think quality over quantity. Look at your employees: Lean on them, draw from them, where they feel that things could be more efficient. Take a look at when you were in crisis mode, through COVID: What did you do without, that you don't have to go back to, because not only did you survive not having 22 steps through a process, and you got it down to, say, 12? Don't go back to the old ways, just because the coast is clear: "Everyone, come out of your storm cellars or your bomb shelters, and go back to your desk. We've survived this mode, but now it's over, and we can put that behind us." When you put that behind you, don't turn around and revert to business as usual. Because that whole landscape has shifted. The market has changed. Again, you've got a choice between reverting to the way the market was—which, let me end the suspense, doesn't exist anymore—or you can reinvent what your market looks like and how you serve it. As you said before, re-evaluate: Are all of these customers truly feeding our why? Are we truly in our genius zone when we work with every single one of the customers we have? If not, then we need to re-evaluate that relationship. Maybe it can be evolved, and maybe it can be changed, but we need to have those conversations.

❝Take the phrase "Because of this pandemic, we need to do more with less" OUT of your vocabulary.❞

BB: I listened to a podcast a while ago, which talked about the new normal in the car industry. Typically, a car sales process has between 7 and 14 steps, including the test drive, the conversation, the "Let me go back and talk to my manager," making you wait while they go find the guy who does all the paperwork and gets the financing and the extended warranty set up, and all that stuff. It's all designed to slow down the process, to be able to maximize profit. But by doing that, moving forward, with all the different options that are available for people to buy a car online, all you're going to do is make people madder and madder and madder. Because guess what? People buying a new car, a lot of times, are moms with young kids or families with young kids. Young kids don't do very well running around a dealership for an hour or two, while mom and dad buy a car. That leads to frustration. So we need to think, "Just because we've always done it this way, because we think we're going to maximize our individual profit on this one deal, maybe we should start thinking about how we maximize the profit on this client over the next 25 years by creating a magical experience?" If we create an efficient, easy process, where people can come in, buy a car, feel excited about it, get the keys and drive away—and then tell every single one of their friends about where they bought the car and the amazing experience that they had—you're going to want to come back to that dealership for service, and you're going to want to come back to buy your next car. If you own the company, you're going to say, "I need to lease 20 cars for the company; maybe I'll come there for our corporate leases as well." We need to start thinking, "Do the policies and the procedures and the way that we've done business in the past really set us up for success in the future?" In a lot of cases, the answer is no. But if we're not asking that question, if we just revert to things how they always were, and assume that "People always accepted this in the past, so they're certainly going to accept it in the future," that's the biggest fallacy. And your competition says, "How can we make this a better customer experience for our clients? I know—we're going to talk to our employees, we're going to talk to their customers, we're going to find out that we can do this." All of a sudden, your business goes over to this other company, because they figured out how to build a better process, to be able to build more loyal customers, because you were afraid to change.

❝We need to start thinking, "Do the policies and the procedures and the way that we've done business in the past really set us up for success in the future?" And in a lot of cases, the answer is no.❞

CC: Loyalty is the key word. We have talked a lot about building connections, not just building better communications. It's so true. We talked earlier about the concept of a sprint mentality versus a marathon mentality. The sprint mentality focuses on the immediate value of a customer; the marathon mentality says, "What's the LIFETIME value?" It may be a slower or longer ramp-up for this customer to become a top-shelf, high-value client, but if you track their value and the value of the relationship over a lifetime, it's the same as this employee loyalty concept: Your loyal employees are going to bring far more value than the lone wolf that you bring in to do a quick strike, and you pay them a lot of money to do one thing, and then they're gone in six months. So it's that lifetime loyalty. Another thing that you just talked about with the car example: This is really an example of how these online car vendors have really stepped up and filled the vacuum in the market, when they said, "We're going to make it ridiculously simple for you to do business with us." They saw a need. We talked about this previously: Why is it that when I already know what car I want to buy, I only test-drive the one, and within a 10-minute test drive I say, "Let's go draw up the paperwork," does it still take you four to six hours to get me out of there with the car? It just can't be like that anymore. Car dealers are a great example of businesses that need to learn from this; they need to step up their game to stay relevant in the market, because there are online vendors that will replace them if they're not. Restaurants have had to figure out a different way during the crisis; when their doors are fully open wide again to receive customers inside, don't forget the lessons and the efficiencies and the additional options for delivery and curbside takeaway that you have invented during this crisis mode. Crises are a great catalyst or leverage point for innovation. What is the thing about a diamond? A diamond is made because it's under tremendous pressure. So look at these industries, these companies and these entities, these individuals who have made diamonds out of the rough. Don't just revert to, "You can only order food from us when you come into the restaurant." Sit your employees down and ask them, and ask your customers, "How can we make doing business with us easier?" It's something that you brought up several episodes ago, and we even talked about on our very first episode: How do we make it "stupid simple" for our clients and our customers to do business with us? How do we make it "stupid simple" for our employees to get their job done, and to connect their very best talents with what we ask them to do every day?

❝Crises are a great catalyst or leverage point for innovation.❞

BB: Now, to bring this back, it all comes down to leadership. It all comes down to leaders who are leading with vision, who are asking, "What can we do to be better? What can we do to move our company and our customers and our employees into the new normal? How can we take the lessons that we've learned, the fact that we've been beaten up a little bit, learn from all these things, and become more effective as a unit, and more valuable to our customers because of this?" Leaders do that. Leaders sit with their people and say, "Let's have a scrum. Let's have a conversation." Whether it's a Zoom communication, whether it's live, whether it's—you pick the technology that you want—but have the ability to say, "What went well? What didn't go well? What did we learn from both?" Let's stop pointing fingers; let's not lay blame. Let's take a look and say, "It's all a learning experience. The money is gone. If we lost a hundred thousand dollars, that bites; but that's money that's invested in the future. That's a $100,000 lesson that allows us to be better moving forward." So we hope that we never do this again, and this is why. This is what we learned from it. These are the policies, procedures and communication we're going to put in place to make sure that it becomes part of our brand story, so that everybody knows that it happened, this is what we've learned from it, and this is how we're going to make sure it doesn't happen again.

CC: It's the whole reason you and I called this series "CREATING the New Normal." We didn't say "reacting" to the new normal; we didn't say "responding" to the new normal. It is incumbent upon smart leaders, or smart companies, that are going to survive and thrive in the future, that they create the new reality around which they build a business, they empower their teams, they serve their customers, and they grow in the future. They've got to create that new reality. And that means they've got to take the right turn toward reinventing, not the left turn toward reverting.

❝It is incumbent upon smart leaders, or smart companies, that are going to survive and thrive in the future, that they create the new reality around which they build a business, they empower their teams, they serve their customers, and they grow in the future.❞

BB: So as we sum this up, what's the biggest thing that we can learn from creating the new normal? Because we do need leaders who are going to lead us into the future. What are the things that we need to be thinking about, as leadership, that will allow us to be successful moving forward, and allow our organizations, our people and our customers to be successful moving forward?

CC: Part of it still comes down to having these types of conversations, quite frankly. We started these conversations, this series, to help leaders pull themselves and their people through this time of unprecedented crisis, but also to remind them that there is a future to build. Their employees are depending upon them to paint the picture of that future. So however long you and I have these conversations, I hope that leaders, and the employees that they are entrusted to lead, continue to have this type of a conversation, whether it's with us or at least with themselves. But the conversation element of this really goes beyond communication, which as we said is different from connection. One of the things we've continued to reinforce throughout this series is the value of the relationship. It's not a contract; it's not an agreement; it's not a "Well, you work for me, and I'm your boss." It's "What type of a relationship can we build that fosters and builds loyalty, that taps into the unique strengths of everyone on the team, and that tangibly shows that connection between your individual why and the company why," however that may have changed through this pandemic? So leaders need to continue to be open to those conversations, create opportunities for those conversations, and be vulnerable in those conversations. Because you will build the future "normal" for your company, your business, and your life together, not in a vacuum.

❝Leaders need to continue to be open to those conversations, create opportunities for those conversations, and be vulnerable in those conversations.❞

BB: Just to add to that, there is no absolute. There is no forever anymore. Our customers are not forever; our employees are not forever; our companies are not forever. The days of people walking into your company at the age of 18 and getting their gold watch at age 65 are no more. There really aren't those types of legacy businesses. There might be a few small types of situations where that exists, but there are very few situations today where employees are with a company 20, 30, 40 years. Companies that have employees for 20, 30, 40 years have figured out how to evolve their employees in a meaningful way, and to say, "Where do you want to be as an employee? What's your vision? What are your goals? What are the things you aspire to?" And they help them get there. That's leadership. As leaders, if we're not waking up every single morning and saying, "How do I make my team better? How do I help people succeed?"—people are going to move on. Whether that's employees, whether that's customers, whether that's businesses as a whole, you either evolve, you change, you look at your processes and say, "This is no longer relevant; why are we still doing this?" or you don't. If you don't, you do it at your own peril. Because all of a sudden, as a company, you become a commodity. You become low-cost, low-value, easily replaced and easily forgotten, your employees move on, and your customers move on. Because you've reverted to where you were, instead of saying, "The world has changed again; how do we change to be relevant with it? How do we make sure our employees understand what those changes are, what it means to them, and how important they are to the future success of this company?" If leaders are not thinking about that all the time, they're not doing their jobs.

66As leaders, if we're not waking up every single morning and saying, "How do I make my team better? How do I help people succeed?"—people are going to move on.99

QUESTION:

You have reached the end of the tunnel; will you turn left or right? Where do you want to go from here? What is the new reality YOU want to create in your business?

_____

_____

_____

_____

_____

_____

_____

_____

_____

What's Next?

As a leader, one of the most important questions you can ask is... "WHAT'S NEXT?"

It is our ability as leaders to keep one eye on the present and the other eye on the horizon that makes us great. Investing the time and effort to see what can be, instead of assuming that what is will always be sufficient, and making the changes necessary to evolve.

With that, we invite you to continue this journey with us.

We have created an exclusive community at

www.leadersmadehere.com

to enable leaders to learn from each other, get inspired, and continue to grow.

JOIN US!

Invite your colleagues and friends who would benefit from enhancing and evolving how they lead. The more people who engage in this journey with us, the richer our future will be.

We look forward to seeing you there.

Ben Baker
www.YourBrandMarketing.com

Claire Chandler
www.ClaireChandler.net

About The Authors

Ben Baker

I help brands tell engaging stories that compel their customers to take action.

For the last 25 years, I have been helping companies communicate with and engage, retain and grow employees. My focus on employee engagement consulting. It is about building leaders, better communication strategies, your brand story and engaging your people in relevant and meaningful ways.

I am a father, a husband, a believer in community, and a passionate teller of the stories of brands. As the founder of Your Brand Marketing, author *of Powerful Personal Brands: a hands-on guide to understanding your* and the host of the three year syndicated YourLIVINGBrand.live show, I work hand in hand with my clients to understand what makes them special and unique in a crowded space. It is by understanding the nuances of a brand, the special things they do that others do not, that unique stories can be told, and audiences engaged.

I am available to consult, provide workshops, and speak on brand, message, market, vision, and value. My goal is always to tell the right story, to the right people, in the right way, so that the intended audience listens, understands, internalizes, engages, and is motivated towards action.

Ben@YourBrandMarketing.com | www.YourBrandMarketing.com

Claire Chandler

I help complex, growing businesses build sustainable, profitable organizations.

I show those organizations how to scale without the growing pains, by finding and fixing the performance bottlenecks that are stifling their growth.

I am the proud wife of a US Marine Corps veteran, and the proud mom of a chinchilla with his own YouTube channel. I believe that the greatest impact on a company's culture is the behavior of its leaders. Drawing on more than 25 years of experience as a people leader, business owner, HR executive and communications strategist, I build leaders who are worthy of being followed.

I work with C-level executives who are ambitious, self-aware and open, and turn them into magnets for the right talent to achieve their mission. If you are ready to become a magnetic leader, reach out.

Claire@TalentBoost.net | www.ClaireChandler.net